PROVERBS 1–9

Readings, A New Biblical Commentary

PROVERBS 1–9

Graham S. Ogden

SHEFFIELD PHOENIX PRESS

2025

Published by Sheffield Phoenix Press
Sheffield Centre for Interdisciplinary Biblical Studies (SCIBS),
University of Sheffield, S10 2TN

www.sheffieldphoenix.com

A CIP catalogue record for this book
is available from the British Library

ISBN 978-1-914490-70-5 (hardback)
ISBN 978-1-914490-71-2 (paperback)

CONTENTS

Author's Preface vii
Acknowledgments ix
Abbreviations xi

PROVERBS 1–9: A COMMENTARY 1
Introduction 1
Date 2
Authorship 3
International Dimension of Wisdom 3
Literary Features 4
A Reading Strategy 6
Wisdom's 'Hope-filled Uncertainty' 8
Outline of Chapters 1–9 11

EXEGESIS 13
Superscription 13
1.1. Proverbs of Solomon, son of David, king of Israel 13
Introduction to Wisdom 14
1.2-7 14
1.8-19 First Address 19
1.20-33 Wisdom Herself Speaks 22

PROVERBS 2 27
2.1-22 Second Address 27
2.1-15 27
2.16-19 31
2.20-22 32

PROVERBS 3 34
3.1-12 Third Address 34
3.13-18 Praising Wisdom 39
3.19-20 Wisdom in Creation 40
3.21-35 Fourth Address 41

PROVERBS 4 47
4.1-9 Fifth Address 47
4.10-19 Sixth Address 49
4.20-27 Seventh Address 52

PROVERBS 5 54
5.1-23 Eighth Address 54
5.1-2 54
5.3-14 55
5.15-20 57
5.21-23 58

PROVERBS 6 60
6.1-19 Wisdom's Warnings 60
6.1-5 Unwise Pledges 60
6.6-11 Contra laziness 62
6.12-15 The Deceiver 63
6.16-19 What the Lord Hates 64
6.20-35 Ninth Address 65

PROVERBS 7 70
7.1-27 Tenth Address 70
7.1-5 Avoid the 'Outsider' Woman 70
7.6-23 The Temptress 71
7.24-27 The Way to Sheol 73

PROVERBS 8 75
8.1-36 Wisdom Speaks Again 75
8.1-3 She Calls 75
8.4-11 Wisdom's Value 76
8.12-21 By me kings rule 77
8.22-31 Wisdom and Creation 79
8.32-36 Finding Life 83

PROVERBS 9 85
9.1-18 Wisdom and Folly 85
9.1-6 Wisdom's House 85
9.7-12 General Maxims 87
9.13-18 Ms Folly 89

POSTSCRIPT 91
The Ecumenicity of Wisdom:
The Book of Proverbs and Confucian Wisdom 91

SELECT BIBLIOGRAPHY 96

Author's Preface

Fifty years ago, I found myself in a doctoral seminar in Princeton studying Qoheleth. That seminar sparked a life-long interest in the biblical Wisdom tradition. Several years later, teaching in Taiwan, appreciating the richness and longevity of the Chinese wisdom traditions only added to that interest, and though I cannot claim any expertise in the latter, the fact that in the Confucian Analects (論語) and in the Daodejing (道德經) one can find multiple examples of identical advice that are completely synchronous with those of ancient Israel and its neighbours, raised again the question of the ecumenicity of the Wisdom tradition, while acknowledging the unique linguistic and cultural contexts of each. In terms of the high status that Christians accorded the biblical text as of 'divine' value, one had to ask, Why was this extra-biblical material not worthy of the same recognition? Wisdom, in every case, biblical or extra-biblical, arises from humans intent on making sense of their lived experiences by deeply reflecting on them, drawing conclusions therefrom, then passing on practical insights gained to the next generations for the individual's and community's well-being.

Wisdom's importance transcends the tribal and national, for it is truly ecumenical. As for the Hebrew Scriptures and ancient Israel's Wisdom tradition, its ecumenical reality defies relegating it to a status inferior to that voted more 'spiritual' and theologically notable; it defies labelling Wisdom as 'secular', over against what is claimed to be 'divinely revealed' spiritual truths. It also defies elevating Biblical Wisdom to a plane higher than that honoured in other ancient cultures and communities simply because of one's view of the Bible as 'God's word'; it defies imposing a Christian teleological agenda on a body of literature that is not concerned with historical matters.

That teleological view imposed upon a co-opted tribal history has been universalized by the Christian church, aided by its integration into the Roman Empire and its spread, especially its spread into Europe. The Hebrew Bible is <u>not</u> the story of all humanity by any stretch of the imagination; rather, it is the story of a small family and its gods that began some

4,000 years ago with Abraham's migration from Haran in modern-day Iraq to Canaan, modern Palestine. The family gradually grew to become a peripatetic tribe that later occupied a region that they claimed God had assigned them (though they never were able to drive out the local inhabitants—see Judges 1). They later formed a short-lived tiny kingdom that was eventually lost to greater neighbouring powers, its descendants finally driven from Judaea and scattered by the Romans in 135 CE. It is a story that belongs exclusively to Abraham's descendants themselves, as do its claims about a God, YHWH, who rescued the family from Egyptian slavery, having 'chosen' it and covenanted with it alone. That private history is not applicable to the global family; it cannot be universalized. Israel's valued history is not the story of China, Japan, Korea, or India, nor of the Mayans, nor of Australia's aborigines, or the Bantu. National or regional histories, religions and cultures are unique, individual and non-transferable.

What <u>is</u> universal is Israel's Wisdom, its sound advice about how best to live locally within the constraints of our shared humanity. Being ecumenical, Wisdom does not focus on what is unique to one tribe's or nation's story, but it concentrates on what is our common human experience. Wisdom defines our options as humans. The book of Proverbs and the other Wisdom material in the Hebrew Bible make no reference to the specific events, personalities or concepts that underpin ancient Israel's other literature. Wisdom's perspective begins and ends with timeless human reflection and considered advice, not with divine revelation claimed in specific acts and events bound to one particular tribal story. Wisdom's counsel must not be relegated, therefore, to some lesser significance if one is seeking a full biblical witness.

This reading will explore Proverb's connections with Chinese wisdom via Confucian texts in demonstration of Wisdom's full ecumenicity.

> *'At fifteen I thought only of study; at thirty I began knowing my place; at forty I was sure of myself; at fifty I was aware of my life under heaven; at sixty I was no longer argumentative; and now at <u>eighty</u> I can follow my heart's desire without offending'.* (子曰：吾十有五而志於學；三十而立；四十而不惑；五十而知天命；六十而耳順；<u>八十</u>而從心所欲；不逾矩)—with apologies to Confucius for updating.

Acknowledgments

I wish to acknowledge my Chinese friends and colleagues, especially in the Bible Society in Taiwan, and Rev. Dr. David Chee in Singapore, for their friendship, encouragement and assistance over the many years spent within their world.

Graham S. Ogden (歐可定)
Ballarat, Vic., Australia
July 2024

Abbreviations

BDB	F. Brown S.R. Driver, and C. Briggs, *A Hebrew and English Lexicon of the Old Testament* (Oxford: Clarendon Press, 1907, repr. 1957)
BHS	*Biblia Hebraica Stuttgartensia* (ed. K. Elliger and W. Rudolph; Stuttgart: Deutsche Bibelstiftung, 1968–77)
ITC	International Theological Commentary
JBL	*Journal of Biblical Literature*
LXX	Septuagint
MT	Masoretic Text
NCBC	New Century Bible Commentary
NICOT	New International Commentary on the Old Testament
NRSV	New Revised Standard Version

PROVERBS 1–9: A COMMENTARY

Introduction

The book of Proverbs represents several collections of Wisdom material known to ancient Israel—1.1–9.18; 10.1–22.16; 22.17–24.22; 24.23-34; 25.1–29.27; 30.1-33; 31.1-31. The first two collections and the fifth are nominally associated with Solomon; the third and fourth are more general and linked with 'the wise' (unidentified); the sixth collection is associated with a non-Israelite Agur son of Jakeh and identified as an oracle (*massa'*) containing his words; the final collection is linked to another foreigner, King Lemuel, also an oracle, one taught to him by his mother. Each collection can be assumed to have once had an independent existence until brought together by the scroll's final Editor.

The completed scroll is located in the Writings, the third section of the Hebrew Bible (*TANAK*). There it stands in company with two other Wisdom documents, the book of Job, and Ecclesiastes/Qoheleth. All three documents, along with some Psalms, present an overview of the role of Wisdom in the life of early Israel and of the tradition's international or ecumenical connections. As a distinct literary genre, Wisdom material, in its several forms, offers its own peculiar perspective on Israel's social and intellectual life, with ramifications for its theological stance.

The phenomenon of Wisdom is not the preserve of any one community; it is a feature of universal humanity and embraces all levels of learning—that of parents teaching children, of artisans teaching practical techniques to their apprentices, of 'professional' Sages giving political and personal counsel to rulers. Wisdom's basic concern is for the individual and community to aspire to the highest of ideals, to find the 'paths' that lead to personal and communal well-being and the development of individual life-skills. In the case of ancient Israel, a theocratic community, the primary goal was defined as finding that mode of living that integrated a lifestyle with knowledge of the Lord (Prov. 1.7), in which awe and knowledge were united. Wisdom is never just an intellectual pursuit; it is intensely practical, an ideal manner of living and working.

The focus for this Reading is Proverbs, chapters 1–9, often thought by some scholars to be the latest component in the collection, but given that the very nature of Wisdom transcends time and place, it is not all that helpful to attempt to date either individual sayings or the several collections that make up the book. What can be said of these initial nine chapters is that they provide a very good introduction to the concerns of Israel's Sages, the nature of their advice, and the various oral and literary forms by which they communicated.

The approach being taken in this reading is to use the literary and rhetorical features of the Hebrew text to expose the meaning of the many sayings found there, to highlight the Sages' advice encouraging audiences to accept and endorse that advice. The Sages could not promise that following their advice would always result in clear and predictable outcomes, so the translation I offer here will use volitional forms of the verbs in order to emphasize the *potential benefit* that Wisdom grants those who follow its path.

Given the ecumenicity of Wisdom, this reading will, where possible, set Chinese examples from Confucius alongside Israelite advice in order to highlight their fundamental similarity, raising inevitable questions as to Wisdom's source within two very different but contemporary cultural worlds.

The LXX text of Proverbs is slightly longer overall than the MT Hebrew text and shows evidence of modifications, suggesting that either it was working from an alternative Hebrew text, or that the Greek translators were supplementing it with additional material. The reading that follows is based on the MT.

This commentary will focus principally on the literary and rhetorical elements in the Hebrew text as the markers that convey its intentions.

Date

Wisdom literature represents the distillation in written form of a cultural group's traditional wisdom, whether as a collection of pithy sayings or an extended narrative, and it is timeless. As a written record, Proverbs presents a final and edited stage in the formulation of ideas and beliefs, of advice based in experiences that have impacted and informed a community over generations. Fixing a date for this finalized form is complex and uncertain because of the nature of the materials that transcend any particular moment in time. One may guess at the date by which the edited composition was completed, but that does not bear any necessary implication for the date of its contents, so discussion of a general and possible date for the book of Proverbs, in part or whole, is ultimately irrelevant. Even Solomon was dependent upon earlier wisdom sayings and advice that had built up over the preceding centuries!

Authorship

Wisdom itself cannot be confined to a certain class or be identified with only one individual. At every level of society, wisdom's practical advice can be and was transmitted—by mothers and fathers who were entrusted with a vital role in educating their children in what makes for a good/ wise citizen, by artisans training their apprentices, as well as by Sages who served as counsellors to royalty and governments. Wisdom arises within and belongs to the historic community rather than being the work or responsibility of one person or group.

While the Superscription in the book of Proverbs identifies Solomon and notes the work itself as his *mᵉšālîm*, it does not mean that Solomon personally wrote or created the material that is included. The Solomonic identification is related to his reputation—problematic though it be—as a Sage, as a collector and author (1 Kgs 4.29-34). It is not possible to isolate any particular saying in this or any other collection and identify it as that of Solomon or some other known Sage. As a Superscript, 1.1 intends to *enhance the reception* of the material here edited as advice consistent with the Solomonic reputation. (See the same heading at 10.1, along with collections attributed to other sages in 22.17; 24.23; 25.1; 30.1 and 31.1.) In other words, authorship of the book of Proverbs cannot be ascribed to an individual, hence the suggested use of *Voice* (*of Wisdom*) when referencing the edited collection. Sages of various backgrounds and periods and through time are responsible for the sayings and advice now accumulated. While there were folk recognized as Sages (Jer. 18.18), whether there was a 'school' or recognized community who taught based on a particular curriculum, as has been proposed by some commentators, there is little in the way of concrete evidence for such in ancient Israel.

International Dimension of Wisdom

Wisdom is not the sole province of any one human community. Every cultural group, large or small, has its accumulated wisdom, a store of knowledge by which it formally and informally educates its citizens. While there may be wisdom elements that seem peculiar to one cultural group, or literary forms that reflect the historic cultural world of that group, there will always be an overlap between the wisdom of all human communities since Wisdom has to do with an approach to practical living as a member of a human community. Whether individual or communal, the wisdom advice of every human gathering suggests a large area of agreement in content and concerns, as well as of forms in which that wisdom is expressed. The wisdom found within the Hebrew Bible is not exclusive but common with that of its neighbours, influencing and being influenced by them, as is evidenced by the foreign materials included here in Proverbs. In the case of Israel, the impact of Egyptian Instructions in particular upon its wisdom tradition is widely acknowledged, even if not applicable in all its details—see the Thirty Sayings in Prov. 22.17–24.22. While the level of contact between Sages throughout the entire region cannot be measured in detail, that it has taken place cannot be denied, as comparative texts make plain. Wisdom in the Hebrew Bible does, however, express that wisdom in the specific context of a relationship to Israel's God, YHWH, for that is its unique experience.

What also is significant is that Israelite Wisdom is 'ahistorical' in the tribal-national sense; it does not refer to any of Israel's historical personalities, or to the historical events and experiences that plot its reported journey. In other words, Wisdom represents a perspective on life that transcends the ideals of a single community and its unique story, for its focus is on broad shared human values. This fact marks Wisdom's perspective as very different from one, such as the Deuteronomic, that presents the Israelite story narrowly in terms of its God Yahweh active in the specific details of its tribal and national life.

Some examples from ancient Chinese wisdom will be included in this commentary to illustrate the ecumenicity of Wisdom's advice, its importance transcending the more limited and potentially divisive sectarian ideologies of the tribal or national. Chinese wisdom as seen in the *Analects of Confucius* presents in terms of the ideal human (君子) in contrast to the 'small person' (小人). See further in the Postscript.

Literary Features

The first feature to note is that throughout these chapters poetic forms dominate, the primary form being the bicolon.

A *Addresses*: The ten addresses each have a generally similar form: (a) they all begin with *b^e^nî*, 'my son' (plural form in 4.10), a very direct address, followed by (b) an imperative—single or multiple, both positive and negative—if negative, the particle *'al* identifies the activities forewarned; (c) the conditional particle *'im*, 'if…', sets out the parameters of a potential situation to be avoided—in the case of 2.1-4 multiple conditions are envisaged; (d) the conditional element may be completed by the apodosis using the *'az* particle, 'then…'; (e) a reason is offered as to why an action is unwise, so we note the use of the explanatory particle *ki*, 'because…'.

B *Speeches*: These are of two kinds: (a) Wisdom (*ḥokmāh*) herself speaks or is spoken about; (b) Warnings are given, as in 6.1-19, against the folly of offering to go surety for someone, against laziness, being a cause of mischief, and anti-social behaviour. Each reflects a noticeable change in the rhetorical form to a more narrative-like style, though still clearly poetic.

C The Addresses and Speeches provide a survey of the *wide range of specialized vocabulary and terminology* that marks all Hebrew Wisdom material.

D Typical of Israelite wisdom's vocabulary is *its black-and-white contrast* between 'the wise' and 'the fool', the latter also spoken of as 'the sinner/wicked/treacherous' in contrast to 'the good/just/upright…'.

E Proverbs 1–9 refers to 'God' only twice in 2.5, in 3.4, and to 'Yahweh' nine times in 1.7, 29; 2.5, 6; nine times in 3.5-33 and six times in chs. 5 to 9. In other words, there is little direct involvement of the divine in the thought and language of these chapters.

F *Imperative verbs* in both positive and negative mode are used throughout to strengthen the advice being offered.

G *Potential Outcomes*: Numerous verbs in the apodosis components of speeches are rendered in NRSV and other translations as simple future tense 'promises'. This situation may be consistent with a Deuteronomic perspective of an assured outcome to one's actions both positive and negative. However, there are many examples—such as 1.28-33 or 2.21-22—in which a rendering as a potential 'may…' would seem more appropriate and consistent with the Sage's recognition that Wisdom's outcomes are often not what one might expect—see below. What appear to be 'promises' are in fact <u>inducements</u> to the young to accept and live by the counsel offered. Consistent with this, I have rendered some of the imperfectives as volitional—e.g., 1.5 *'Let the wise one…*; 'or as in 2.16 '*May you be saved from…*'.

H *Wisdom as a way of life* rather than an intellectual exercise is the focus of 2.8-20 with a concentration of the parallel metaphors of a 'path' and 'way', also 4.10-19.

- I *A numerical form (x, x+1)*, one of many unique wisdom forms, is exemplified in 6.16-19. See further in the Postscript re Chinese wisdom's use of similar numerical forms.
- J In 8.22-31 a series of *temporal phrases* is applied to emphasize the pre-creation context in which Wisdom participated as agent in Yahweh's creation of the world. With 3.19-20 it reveals the world-view that underpins Israel's Wisdom movement. That paradigm of Wisdom as the agent of God's creative work in Proverbs has another and much later significant application; it is the paradigm for 'the word' in John 1.1.
- K In the Hebrew worldview as noted in Proverbs, Wisdom, *ḥokmāh*, is personified and given a female instructor role. Wisdom here is a created 'being', but not just a created being; rather, Wisdom is said to have been the very *first*—whether in terms of order or significance—of God's creative acts (Prov. 8.22-31), such that Wisdom then became the *agent* by which God 'established' the earth and the heavens (Prov. 3.19-20). Wisdom as the precursor to Creation itself was a highly imaginative way of elevating its significance in Israel's intellectual tradition. In Confucian thought, Wisdom is never personified; it is a set of values for a manner of living to be acquired by attending to wise instruction. That life-style should grant its own reward.
- L There is no scholarly consensus regarding the possible origin of the notion of Wisdom as a woman. That the idea lies within Israel's pre-exilic and syncretistic religious world, or is merely some poetic and literary device, are two possibilities. However, what can be said is that Lady Wisdom in chapters one and eight stands as the antithesis of the Foolish Woman in 2.16-19; 5.1-6; 6.24-26; 7.16-23, against whose wiles the young are being warned.

A Reading Strategy

Gerhard von Rad's *Old Testament Theology*, a 2-volume work, published in 1957 (ET 1962), gave no place to Wisdom material for it could not be made to fit within his Christian theological paradigm, though ten years later he did write a separate work in which to discuss Wisdom. The Christian paradigm von Rad adopted was of a God active in Israel's history with teleological purpose (*Heilsgeschichte*), namely, to rescue humanity from Adam's sin. The paradigm takes Paul's Adam-Jesus contrast (Romans 5; 1 Cor. 15.22, 45) and seeks to historicize the mythical Adam with a claim that the Bible has an over-arching intentionality, a *telos*, from a beginning in a Creation myth (Gen. 3) to a conclusion in the life and death of Jesus. Second century CE Christianity created this longitudinal reading strategy that was alien and unknown to ancient Israel. It was further developed in Anselm's eleventh-century CE theory that an historicized Adam's sin affects every rational human being, only to be resolved in Jesus' sacrificial death. Ancient Israel's reading of its Scriptures, however, was atomistic, with *torah* its only unifying notion; its contents usually were only ever heard, as selections were read publicly by one of the tiny minority who had access to a scroll and who was literate, or when shared orally by a passing storyteller. In an essentially oral community, any hand-written text was of extremely limited availability and very restricted public access. Yes, there was a recognized list of individual scrolls, but no cohesive and overarching organizing principle other than the three-part division of Torah/Law, Prophets and Writings (*TANAK*).

The Christian teleological reading strategy created and imposed on the Hebrew Scriptures was only possible once (1) all the individual scrolls had been brought together into a one-volume codex, (2) read in a new fixed order that concluded the Hebrew material with the Prophets instead of 2 Chronicles in the Writings, (3) new materials were created and added in the post-Jesus years to offer its new sectarian perspective on that Hebrew text. Only then, around the end of the second century CE, was there a notion of a single volume whole 'Bible', a notion that yet remains in dispute between the churches east and west as to its exact contents. Codex Sinaiticus from the fourth century CE is our earliest extant example of such a codex, but it contains more Hebrew 'books' in its Greek translation than does the MT text, the earliest of which we access in the Leningrad Text of the tenth century CE. It took many centuries before 'The Bible' was a meaningful entity available to a wide audience, and allowing it to be (mis)read teleologically.

Then there is the view that the Wisdom material is/was a 'secular' product—a view exemplified by William McKane—because sourced from human experiences and from one's reflective process. This particular notion has meant that Wisdom holds minimal interest for a Christian theology that emphasized divine revelation and its claimed certainties, that prioritized God's claimed role in the historic events involving his 'chosen' people—i.e., God calling Abraham, leading the Exodus, gifting the land of Canaan etc. The view that Wisdom in the Hebrew Scriptures is 'secular' or non-religious, non-spiritual, and therefore of far less theological significance, is one that rests on a 'western' notion of the separation of the secular from the religious—Webster's dictionary defines 'secular' as *unconnected to any religious or spiritual pursuit*—a false bifurcation in the case of ancient theocentric Israel, as Prov. 1.7 makes plain. Israel's Sages were thoroughly integrated into their theocratic world, their theological ideas basic to their manner of instructing and advising the younger generations as to how they should best live within their community. Dismissing Wisdom, therefore, as 'secular', as though it is of such less value, demeans both Wisdom and Theology.

It has also been traditional among many scholars to speak of Wisdom Theology as 'Creation Theology', to honour the Lord as Creator (Eccl. 12.1), to link social order to the cosmic order, to highlight the establishment of Wisdom as God's first pre-Creation act. While this perspective may be helpful in locating Wisdom within Israel's overall thinking (Eccl. 12.1; Ps. 104), it is perhaps more cogent to read the purpose and function of the two references in Prov. 3.19-20 and 8.22-31 as elevating Wisdom itself, its own role and importance in one's dealing with life, rather than a more general focus on the natural world and on God as Creator.

The Israelite Wisdom material does not concern itself with any reference to the Israelite story, its special events, its leading personalities, or its fundamental concepts; its focus is elsewhere, in practice rather than in ideology. The book of Proverbs, as an example, clearly belongs in a different genre with its own peculiar worldview that does not centre about claimed divine acts in ancient Israel's history. The reading offered here will aim to keep the book of Proverbs well within its ancient cultural and historical Hebrew context, to prioritize its literary and rhetorical evidence, while acknowledging the ecumenicity of <u>all</u> Wisdom. Confucian Wisdom will be considered to illustrate this latter further.

Wisdom's 'Hope-filled Uncertainty'

One theological frame of considerable significance in the Hebrew Bible is that found in its Deuteronomic materials, i.e., the book of Deuteronomy and the Deuteronomistic History, Joshua–2 Kings. These intensely nationalistic materials reflect a simple black-and-white theology of blessings for obedience and curses for disobedience with respect to the commandments. Those said blessings and curses are all spelled out in totally materialistic terms—see Deut. 27.1–28.68. The link between material gain and obedience is guaranteed in the Deuteronomic worldview as Yahweh blesses and rewards those who obey *Torah* and curses those who don't. The material found in the book of Proverbs <u>appears</u> to be rooted in this same Deuteronomic approach to life, for God is said to reward the wise who live by wisdom's values (see e.g., Prov. 2.21-22; 3.1-10, 27-33; 8.32-36…). Over against this is Wisdom's belief that an individual's actions themselves have their own potential outcomes, be it reward or disaster.

Perhaps there were some 'teachers' who simplified their instruction and advice in order to make a point clearer, parents who taught their children in black-and-white terms that suited their own domestic context. However, the Wisdom movement was not so monolithic that it did not have within it those who had a more mature understanding of the human situation and offered advice or counsel that was appropriate, and conditional; not everything about the human experience could be so simply taught. A Sage like Qoheleth was not the only member of Israel's Wisdom community who saw, questioned, and then concluded that everything about the human experience was *hevel*, an enigma, that it was and remained beyond neat human solutions. As Confucius noted: 'Life and death are determined by fate, riches and honour are fixed by Heaven' (…死生有命，富貴在天). That awareness, that recognition was the mark of the real Sage, knowing and admitting to Wisdom's limitations when confronting many human issues, agreeing that there was something deeply troubling when God's inscrutable ways were sought, but anticipated rewards either were not forthcoming, or seemed often to go to the 'wrong' people, the undeserving (see Eccl. 3.16-22; 4.1-4 etc.). The author(s) of Job used the three friends' dialogue in chapters 3–25 as a vehicle inserted into an original story in order to dismiss the strict Deuteronomic thesis, for Job's suffering was indiscriminate and totally unrelated to his actions and lifestyle. After all, Job was judged to be one 'sinless and upright, who feared God and turned away from evil' (Job 1.1), yet suffer he did, losing everything while somehow managing to hold on to his faith in his God. And if it is true that the basic story of Job has possible Edomite roots, then its perspective is all the more valuable for the study of theology in ancient Israel and of Wisdom in particular.

What then might be the main theological perspective of the book of Proverbs within Israel's Wisdom tradition? For this reader the answer begins with the interpretation and translation of many of the Hebrew verb forms used throughout since they appear to be 'promises' regarding life-style outcomes. For example, in 1.19 there is a thoroughly generalized statement that NRSV renders '…such is the end(?) of all who are greedy for gain, it *takes away* the life of its possessors', where the verb represents what was widely believed to be true, but never could such an outcome be guaranteed. Understanding the verbal form as volitional, as expressing a wish, '*may it take away…*', is more in keeping with wise advice. Rendering it as a clear and certain promise, as in NRSV, leaves the impression that 'death' or 'loss of life' is always and unquestionably the result of folly, when it is not. No Sage worthy of the title would be so foolish as to guarantee the outcome of any specific action, unless hyperbole (false promises?) was a deliberate educational device, and so understood by the recipients of the counsel.

So, how should these imperfect verb forms in Proverbs be understood? They clearly are not prescriptive or predictive. However, the counsel or instruction offered citizens needed to have sufficient urgency or imperative thrust, inducements, for its counsel and advice to be taken seriously. So, the question comes down to the syntax of the imperfect forms of the Hebrew verb, the completed or incomplete nature or state of the action. It is important therefore that calls to learn, to live by the advice offered, and potential outcomes for the individual envisaged by the Sage, should be expressed by 'let/may/might/could/should' and similar auxiliaries to conform to their volitional intent. Translators need seriously to consider what rendering is appropriate in order to preserve the note of *potentiality* that is intrinsic to all sage advice. This would then ensure that Wisdom's advice was seen as absolutely independent of any Deuteronomic absolutism.

Wisdom's advice is always relative and contextual, advising what is 'best' or 'better' for a given situation, a perspective grounded in the uncertainty engendered in our human experience. As Confucius said with respect of knowledge: 'It is to know both what one knows and what one does not know' (知之爲知之，不知爲不知，是知也). Wisdom thus offers a theology bound in 'mystery' since Israel's Yahweh and his ways, though keenly sought, were ultimately inscrutable. Questions abound for the Sage, but absolute answers are often elusive, hence the 'better/best' limitation. Yahweh was believed to be beneficent, but allowance had always to be made for exceptions since God's ways are ultimately unknowable (Eccl. 2.14-17; 8.14-16; 9.11-12). That is the Wisdom reality, and it must be taken seriously. Furthermore, Hebrew Wisdom's worldview was this-worldly; birth and death are the boundaries within which its positive contribution to one's lived experience rests. Projecting any resolution to a post-death 'heaven' is beyond Wisdom's purview (Eccl. 3.18-22).

In a world deemed by the Sages to be uncertain, can one find Hope? The challenge for Wisdom lay in retaining a belief in divine beneficence. If Wisdom believed that it was not possible ultimately to access the intricacies of the mind of God, then any positive 'reward' from following Wisdom's advice could only be seen as potential—yet therein lie also the seeds of Hope! One avenue for possibly resolving the Uncertainty issue was the 'restoration' of whatever had been lost—to resurrect the just (2 Macc. 7.14), to give back what had been taken away. Only then could the Sages maintain faith in God's essential justice and beneficence, *even if they could not declare when or if* such restoration might happen. Job received back all that had been taken from him, and more—see Job 42.10-17. Without that vital ending, the message of the book of Job has little theological significance other than as a debate about Deuteronomic theory.

Wisdom can be said, therefore, to represent a very nuanced theology, one different from that of the strict Deuteronomic outlook, and different again from a 'traditional' Christian reading that obsesses about Sin. Wisdom theology is a theology that cannot be absolute; it is very conscious of divine inscrutability and thus of its own limitations and parameters. Israelite Wisdom offers what I would call a '*hope-filled uncertainty*', a positive theology, but one that is very discomforting to those who look for or demand closed theological certainty. Wisdom offers benefits and hope to any who attend, yet it remains conditional, contextual and uncertain. Does that not ultimately define Faith?

Outline of Chapters 1–9

- 1.1 Superscript
- 1.1-7 Introduction to Wisdom
  - 1.8-19 *First Address*
  - 1.20-33 Wisdom Herself Speaks
  - 2.1-22 *Second Address*
  - 3.1-12 *Third Address*
  - 3.13-18 In Praise of Wisdom
  - 3.19-20 Wisdom in Creation
  - 3.21-35 *Fourth Address*
  - 4.1-9 *Fifth Address*
  - 4.10-19 *Sixth Address*
  - 4.20-27 *Seventh Address*
  - 5.1-23 *Eighth Address*
  - 6.1-19 Wisdom's Warnings
    - 6.1-5 Unwise Pledges
    - 6.6-11 Contra Laziness
    - 6.12-15 The Deceiver
    - 6.16-19 What the Lord Hates
  - 6.20-35 *Ninth Address*

7.1-27	*Tenth Address*	
	7.1-5	Avoid the Outside Woman
	7.6-23	The Temptress
	7.24-27	The Way to Sheol
8.1-36	Wisdom Speaks Again	
	8.1-3	Wisdom Calls
	8.4-11	Wisdom's Value
	8.12-21	By Me Kings Rule
	8.22-31	Wisdom and Creation
	8.32-36	Finding Life
9.1-18	Wisdom and Folly	
	9.1-6	Wisdom's House
	9.7-12	General Maxims
	9.13-18	Ms Folly

As is clear, these opening chapters of the book of Proverbs are dominated by two different literary forms—one, a series of Addresses offering advice to the younger generation, the other as Speeches by and about Wisdom itself. The ten Addresses are instructions directed at an audience identified as 'my son/child' (*b*^{e}*nî)*, a phrase that could be personal, that of a father speaking to his child, or more general, as that of a teacher to a pupil. The six Speeches relate to the role of Wisdom personified as a woman who herself speaks, or about whom special qualities are identified (1.20-33; 3.13-20; 8.1-36). These are all prefaced by the Superscript in 1.1 that identifies the contents of the Book as associated in some manner with Solomon, followed by a definition of Wisdom and its function (1.2-7).

It is quite evident that these nine chapters that begin the book of Proverbs constitute an Editor's selection of materials, both oral and written, representative of ancient Israel's traditional Wisdom. The one addressing the younger generations, i.e., the book's nominal Speaker, is what I have called the *Voice of Wisdom*; it is not the personal advice of one individual, Solomon or any other. The *Voice* represents the Israelite community's centuries of accumulated knowledge and teachings. Its advice is expressed in both positive form, by way of jussive verbs, as well as warnings by way of negative imperatives. The *Voice* offers a rounded set of traditional principles by which one should aspire to live—what one should actively pursue, as well as what one should actively reject.

Exegesis

Superscription

1.1. Proverbs of Solomon, son of David, king of Israel

This book title has been provided by the editor of the collection, using the generic term *māšāl* to characterize its contents. The Solomonic identification is related to his renown as a Sage and author (1 Kgs 4.29-34). However, as a Superscript, the editor's purpose in 1.1 is assumed to be to enhance the reception of the material, here edited as advice consistent with the Solomonic reputation. In terms of the MT, it presumably represents one collection, chapters 1-9 only, as there is another 'title' at 10.1; further collections associated with other individuals are found at 22.17, 24.11, 25.1, 30.1 and 31.1. However, there is also the possibility that the Superscript is intended as a title for the entire body of collected sayings, meaning that the phrase is merely a formal editorial Introduction.

Rendering the term *māšāl*, one of numerous wisdom forms, as 'proverb', is limiting given its more narrow sense in English where it simply approximates the Hebrew bicolon that contrasts wise and foolish action—as in Prov. 10.1-32, for example. The noun *māšāl* as used here is best viewed as a generic term, for examples throughout the Hebrew Bible indicate its very broad application—from short sayings to more extended poems, and with a variety of functions. In Ezek. 17.2, for example, it refers to a parable or allegory, in Ps. 44.15 it is a taunt song. The most one can say about the noun is that it has a broad semantic range within the general area of poetic discourse, mostly confined to instructional material. Some commentators have sought to link the noun *māšāl* to the verb *māšal*, 'to rule'. However, the connection is linguistically opaque, to say the least, and the attempt fails to consider the noun as a homograph with its own unique identity.

The genitive phrase *mišlē šᵉlōmōh* identifies the collection as having some relationship with Solomon, though the nature of that connection is not defined other than being related to the king's broad reputation. Was he responsible for writing or for collecting the range of sayings that follow? Nothing in the text allows the question to be answered beyond its function as an editorial literary device.

Identifying Solomon as 'son of David' seems unnecessary as the very name 'Solomon' would have been universally recognized, especially given his reputation as a wise king. The additional phrase, 'king of Israel', likewise is hardly required for identification, so perhaps it has some other purpose such as the editor wanting to elevate the value of the collection by giving Solomon's full pedigree at the beginning of the collection. The 'king of Israel' phrase is also ambiguous, applicable to both Solomon and David as rulers of the united Israel.

Introduction to Wisdom

1.2-7

> *In order to know wisdom and instruction, to comprehend words of understanding.*
> *In order to acquire instruction in wise dealing, righteousness, justice, and uprightness.*
> *In order to endow the simple with shrewdness, the young with knowledge and discretion.*
> *Let the wise one take note and increase in learning, and may the discerning acquire skill.*
> *In order to understand a proverb and a figure of speech, the words of the wise and their riddles*
> *'Fear of the Lord' is the first step in (gaining) knowledge; wisdom and instruction (are what) fools despise.*

The decision to include v. 7 as integral to the text unit is based on the three-term inclusio, *da'ath*, *ḥokmāh*, *mūsār*, in v. 2 and v. 7. It is v. 7 that concludes the section and is its main statement, with the dependent infinitives and jussives leading to that fundamental Israelite motto that outlines its concept of Wisdom. Syntactically, vv. 2-7 form a discrete and independent unit, a statement as to the instructional purpose of the collected material, and of the nature of Wisdom in general (v. 7).

Introducing the unit with a series of infinitive construct verb forms with the *l*^{e}-preposition expressing purpose or goal, combined with the wide range of related wisdom terms is an unusual rhetorical feature of this book. The use of two jussive verbs in v. 5 seems to intrude into those purposive infinitive sequences—it could mean that v. 5 should introduce the unit, but there is no textual justification for that reordering. This reading will proceed on the assumption that the unit overall represents a call to all Israelites, no matter of what age or class, to grow in Wisdom in its many aspects.

At the literary level, vv. 2-4 consist of three half verses (vv. 2a, 2b, 3a) each beginning with infinitives relating to wisdom's purpose, and a statement regarding Israelite ethical values (v. 3b), followed by two additional infinitives addressing 'the simple' and 'the young', two quite specific audiences, though they may well overlap. Verse 5 uses two jussive verbs—'listen' and 'acquire'—addressed to 'the wise one', a seemingly different and more mature audience, followed by the infinitive calling them 'to understand', i.e., learn more about, a variety of wisdom's literary forms. The climactic v. 7 refers to the foundation of Israelite wisdom. It is a warning to the fools who fail to recognise that truth, and to any who would belittle wisdom's importance.

While commentators usually link these six verses syntactically with v. 1, this reader suggests that the Superscript is just that, an editor's independent nominal clause as his introduction to these chapters. Over against this, vv. 2-7 represent a statement of Wisdom's general purpose, expressed largely in these infinitives; the infinitives are not especially to be linked with Solomon's *mᵉšālîm* in 1.1 as they identify Wisdom's overall purpose. This means that vv. 2-4 focus on the basic wisdom instruction of the 'simple' and the 'young', with vv. 5-6 constituting a call to 'the wise' also to gain *more* knowledge of the formal elements such as proverbs, figures of speech, sayings of the wise, and riddles. There does seem to be a different context in view in vv. 5-6 that suggests two slightly different audiences. Such a reading fits with the overall structure of Proverbs 1–9, with ten specific Addresses that counsel *my son(s)*, i.e., the younger generation, in basic practical wisdom, with the more expanded commentary about Wisdom herself in chapters 8-9 aimed at the wise who are called to seek even deeper knowledge.

As for the taxonomy of the nine Hebrew terms relating to aspects of wisdom that feature in these verses, English language renderings offered are varied, indicating that modern definitions of the ancient terms may not equate so precisely. One can only project from the word-root involved in each term or phrase and consider the context of these various examples found throughout the book. However, the specific nuance of each ancient Hebrew term may inevitably escape modern translators and readers.

da'ath:	knowledge, learning
ḥokmāh:	wisdom (generic)
mūsār:	instruction, discipline

'imrē bînāh:	words of insight/discernment
haskēl:	wise dealing, intelligence, success
'ormāh:	shrewdness, prudence
m^{e}*zimmāh:*	discretion, foresight, guidance
leqaḥ:	insight, learning
ṭaḥbulôth:	skills (practical)

The degree to which each of these terms might overlap or be distinctive—and who knows exactly what taxonomic distinctions might have been made within that ancient society?—is less important than that they together mark the breadth of field that Hebrew practical wisdom encompassed.

1.2 Both halves of the verse are introduced by infinitives with the preposition *l*^{e} attached. The first item in the list of infinitives is *lāda'ath*, literally '(in order) to know', or 'for the knowing of…' as the Hebrew infinitives can be compared to English gerunds.

The objects of each half verse are parallel, so knowing 'wisdom and instruction' is parallel to comprehending 'sayings of insight', both referring to aspects of the teachings of the Wisdom tradition. In this way readers are introduced immediately to the topic and purpose of the collection: it is to provide basic instruction in *ḥokmāh*, the most common word for 'wisdom', in *mūsār*, 'instruction', and a keyword in Proverbs 1–9, as well as in *'imrē bînāh*, 'sayings giving insight'. Each of the three objects can be considered generic.

1.3 Here the focus is on acquiring (*lāqaḥ*) or receiving 'instruction' (*mūsār*), further defined as what can make one more aware of issues—the infinitive *haskēl* suggests gaining 'insight' or making one more aware.

The scope of the *mūsār*, a key term throughout Proverbs, is identified in v. 3b as involving three moral qualities—righteousness, justice and uprightness. Righteousness (*ṣedeq*) speaks of being fair and just in treating others; justice (*mišpāṭ*) has more of the connotation of living according to *Torah*; uprightness (*m*^{e}*šārîm*) comes from a root that indicates something straight and in a moral sense acting always in the right way, as defined by wisdom. These are practical qualities, as distinct from the more abstract notions in v. 2, making it obvious that wisdom is not just an intellectual pursuit, but includes the manner in which one approaches everyday life. In Confucian terms, there are three very similar concepts—仁義 (benevolence), 公平 (justice/fairness), 正值 (uprightness)—as required values.

Teaching the simple to become shrewd and knowing (*'ormāh*), is another of wisdom's goals (v. 4). Those described as 'simple ones' (*p*ᵉ*tā'yim*) are not being slighted for their IQ but are identified as ones who are rather naïve, easily (mis)led. The adjective can have both positive and negative connotations, but in this context *'ormāh* is one of Wisdom's gifts (see also 8.5) that can equip a person with strategies to defend against any who would seek to take advantage.

As well as assisting the simple, youth generally can benefit from wisdom's gift of knowledge and *m*ᵉ*zimmāh*, 'discretion', the ability to discern, to successfully navigate situations, i.e., a very practical skill that many young persons lack because of limited life experience.

The focus of the verse on the naïve and inexperienced demonstrates the key role that Wisdom sought to play in assisting the younger generation acquire the life-skills required for a meaningful personal and community experience.

1.5-6 As noted above, v. 5 opens with a jussive form that calls for the wise person to listen up, together with a call to increase (*yôsep*) or grow in respect of practical skills. This latter (*leqaḥ*) is a rare word, essentially limited to the Proverbs collection. Addressing the wise one—*ḥākām* is generic—in this manner implies that it is directed at those other than the simple and youth. It is set alongside the call for the wise/discerning one to acquire skills, practical skills (*taḥbulôth*) related to wisdom—it is a rare word with a possible nautical background where ropes were used, here as a metaphor. This is explained as a deeper understanding of several wisdom literary forms—apart from the *māšāl*, figures of speech (*m*ᵉ*lîṣāh*), words of the wise, and riddles (*ḥîdothām*) are specified (see also 9.9).

The change from infinitive verbs in vv. 2-4 to the jussive forms in v. 5 is difficult to explain on syntactic grounds, but if two different audiences—the young/simple, and the sage—are being addressed separately, then it may be accepted. Both groups are drawn together in the unit's closing statement in v. 7.

1.7 This initial unit concludes with the well-known statement or article of faith—*The fear of the Lord is the beginning of knowledge* (NRSV). It is often quoted as the most appropriate description of Israelite Wisdom. Before analyzing this statement, it is salutary to recall that ancient Israel was a theocratic community in which the claimed covenant relationship of Yahweh with Israel was foundational; all life, religious and 'secular', circulated around the belief that Israel's God, Yahweh, was the people's primary point of reference. Cultic, social, practical and justice concerns,

Torah, all had to relate in some manner to Yahweh's assumed place as the nation's lord and master, its *'ādôn*. It was inevitable that Israel's Wisdom movement and Wisdom's role should be expressed in terms of the divine overlord.

The verse itself is a good example of the bicolon, the two-line saying that contrasts the wise and the foolish. This particular literary form is not often used in chapters 1–9, but is the dominant form in chapters 10–22.

The phrase *the fear of the Lord* (*yir'ath yhwh*) is a genitive construction that can have two close but different senses: it can refer to *the awesomeness of the Lord himself* or, as an objective genitive, refer to *one's attitude of awe shown towards the Lord.* It is the latter sense that almost universally dominates commentary. Whichever interpretation one prefers, it is Israel's Yahwistic worldview that provides the context in which Israelite Wisdom operated. It has nothing to do with intelligence; it is purely an attitude of mind with respect of YHWH, the national God.

The statement that awe is the beginning (*rē'šîth*) of knowledge uses the term noted in Gen. 1.1, 'In the beginning, God…', clearly there a temporal sense. In Prov. 1.7 that sense is modified to become one of priority, meaning that without a healthy respect for Yahweh, knowledge/wisdom is not possible. It is a sweeping statement of first principles that is Israelite wisdom's cultural and theological starting point. It also makes implicit that if there is a beginning, then there must be on-going learning as emphasized in v. 5. Wisdom is a process of live growth, of maturing, not an end in itself. As a manner of living, it can expect to have its own rewards in the here and now.

The question to be asked is, 'What is the nature of the relationship between Wisdom's advice and Awe of Yahweh?' How do they interrelate? Does 'awe' imply a state of quivering fear that drives one to act in a particular, compliant way? Or is it a matter of one acknowledging that by learning to follow wisdom's advice one comes to know something more about Yahweh, to appreciate Yahweh's awesomeness? The sense is rather vague, but there are other similar references to 'fear of the Lord' in Proverbs—9.10 suggests that 'the first principle (*tᵉḥillāh*) of wisdom itself is 'fear of Yahweh' and knowledge of the holy one is 'insight'; in 15.33 it is 'fear…is instruction in wisdom', similar to Job 28.28—indicating that a sage's advice as to how to live and thrive in Israel's theocratic community is totally integrated with one's attitude to Yahweh. These varied expressions emphasize that one who lives wisely, following wisdom's advice, is thereby demonstrating fear or respect for Yahweh.

In contrast to the wise, the foolish who do not prioritize wisdom's advice are said to despise it, showing no 'fear' or respect for the Lord and his authority. The binary contrast that characterizes the vocabulary used in the world of Israelite wisdom is here on display: 'wise' equates to 'good'; 'fool' equates to 'wicked'; intellectual and moral are thus mutually defining in this national worldview.

1.8-19. First Address

Listen, my child, to your father's instruction and do not reject your mother's teaching;
For they are a beautiful garland for your head and pendants for your neck.
My child, if lawless individuals should entice you, do not yield;
If they say, "Come with us, let us lie in wait to spill some blood; let us ambush an innocent person;
Let us 'swallow' them alive, as does Sheol, completely like those who go down into the Pit.
We may find all kinds of precious treasure and fill our houses with the loot.
Throw your lot in with us; we can share the purse between us."
My child, do not walk in the way with them, refuse to tread their paths,
For their feet run to evil, and they are quick to shed blood.
"To bait the net while the bird is looking is useless,"
Yet they lie in wait to shed their own blood, they set an ambush for their own lives.
Such is the path of everyone who pursues greedy gain; it takes away the life from any who have it.

This First Address is a well-constructed and balanced unit with the themes of 'lying in wait to shed blood' and 'ambush' from v. 11 repeated in v. 18, contrasting 'walk' in v. 15 with 'run' in v. 16. It also points to the fate of the innocent victim in v. 11 becoming the fate of those who perpetrate the violence (vv. 18-19). The repetition serves as a form of inclusio that marks the unit.

The *Voice* calls to the young generation with a solemn warning; it is in three parts, each beginning with the address 'my child'. First are the imperatives that place parental instruction at the forefront—a father's instruction and a mother's *torah* (1.8-9). Balancing the two imperatives—the first in positive and the second in negative mode—makes clear the importance attached to parental guidance.

Part Two of the Address, vv. 10-14, introduces an example of a potential temptation facing the young. It is expressed as a conditional, a potential hazard that might be offered a young and innocent person urged to join in some anti-social behaviour for material and ill-gotten gain. The contrast between the positive contribution of the parent and the totally negative action of the 'sinner' is a deliberate rhetorical device.

In Part Three, vv. 15-19, the *Voice* issues another warning, pointing out that the fate of the victim in Part Two will become the fate of any who follow the path of anti-social or violent acts.

1.8 The call to 'Hear…!' asks for more than just listening, for the verb *šāma'* also expects a positive response, taking on board what is spoken of, hence it also implies 'Obey…!'. In Chinese the advice is similar, the verb 聽 is not only to hear, but 'to obey/follow.'

The parental role in informing and shaping a child's education for life is/was crucial to the child's full participation in the life and work of the community. The 'father' and 'mother' roles here could well be considered metaphors for more formal teachers, but the literal sense is probably intended—see also 6.20. The use of *tōrāh* in respect of the mother's instruction suggests its more general or broad sense of 'teaching', rather than the narrow use as 'Law'.

1.9 The beautiful adornment and the necklace (*'ănāqîm*) in v. 9 are here metaphors for things of high value. The 'gracious garland' (*liwyat ḥēn*) is a rare term and in v. 9a refers to a form of headwear that recognizes the honoured position or achievement of an individual. Here and in 4.9 are its only occurrences. It may apply to a male or female; v. 9b the necklace would seem to apply more to a female, though in Judg. 8.26 it is a decorative item around a camel's neck! Whether this kind of male-female distinction is intended is uncertain since the formal address is directed only to 'my child', masculine singular, but as such it is a broad inclusive reference. The point, surely, is that by paying attention to parental instruction, any child is receiving something of great value.

1.10-12 Part Two of the Address, vv. 10-14, raises the surprizing possibility of a young person being enticed to participate in a cowardly attack upon an innocent victim. The suggestion for violence comes from those described as 'sinners', a Wisdom code word for the foolish. The example itself seems outrageous and highly unlikely, but readers need not make general assumptions about society at the time.

The *Voice* presents the case-study using two phrases 'lying in wait' and 'ambush'. The two phrases are used as a type of inclusion for the section, being repeated in v. 18. The mention of 'blood' implies that they intend to murder the victim and rob him or her, and the attack is described as a wanton one (*ḥinnām*), lacking any justification. Two similes are used to illustrate the goal of the attack by comparing their intended actions to that of burial. It uses the traditional notions of Sheol, the place of departed spirits, and the Pit, i.e., the grave. Comparing the opening up of a grave site to accept a corpse with their intention to metaphorically 'swallow' the victim is a colourful metaphor (see also Num. 16.30).

1.13-14 It is possible to read the verbs as continuing the volitional or cohortative verbs in vv. 11-12 with the sinners' further invitation to 'find' all manner of expensive items (*hôn yāqār*) for their own private enjoyment. The verb 'find' (*māṣā'*) clearly does not mean locating something lost, but rather is code, in this example, for robbing homes of the more wealthy in the community, to acquire valuable objects for themselves. Having stolen these goods, they then plan to 'fill' their own homes with the plunder, implying theft on a grand scale.

To encourage the young to consider this possible invitation, the sinners offer to share the loot equally. To have 'one purse' means that all loot will be placed 'in the middle' and made subject to the drawing of lots (*gôrāl*) to guarantee fairness in their distribution. This closes the imaginary offer of the sinners.

1.15-19 In this third section of the first address the *Voice* resumes, warning the child against 'walking' in the way of the sinners. It uses several rhetorical elements—a contrast between walking and running; a repeat of the 'lying in wait' and 'ambush' imagery from v. 11; applying the fate of the innocent victim in v. 11 to any who would follow the way of the sinner. It also includes a cryptic proverb-like form in v. 17 that can serve as a fulcrum around which the advice circles, with v. 18 offering the conclusion to be drawn.

The parallel terms 'way' (*derek*) and 'path' (*n^{e}tîbāh*) in v. 15 introduce paired metaphors common to proverbial wisdom that likens one's life to a 'walk' or journey—see e.g., 2.7-20; 3.7; 4.11-19. The Confucian texts use the same metaphors (道, 路), defining the person of virtue to be on a three-lane path or way, those being: benevolence （仁）, wisdom （智慧）and courage (勇).

The wording of v. 16 appears also within Isa 59.7 with only minor disparities so there has been some discussion as to the priority of the one over the other. It is a pointless exercise since the date of the proverbial material cannot be determined, and in any event, there is always the possibility that the expression was widely known, even if only recorded twice in the Hebrew text.

It is the cryptic quotation in v. 17 that is of more interest since its interpretation and intention is uncertain, along with its place within the advice being offered. First to note is that the phrase *ba'al kānāph* for a bird occurs only here and in another Wisdom book, Eccl. 10.20. So, does the bird reference apply to the thugs, and is the 'net' a trap for them? It appears to mean that it is foolish to set a trap for a bird if it can see the trap being set up, but that way of reading assumes that the bird knows about such matters and will not be caught, a rather implausible conclusion. The phrase 'in vain' (*ḥinnām*) points to human action, so perhaps in its context here it refers to pointless action related to the ambush of an innocent passer-by. The one who actually will be caught is not the intended victim but the one who sets the trap. This then highlights the point in v. 18 that the ones planning the attack, the sinners, are the ones who will suffer the consequences of their own actions, namely the loss of their *nepheš*, life-force (心命); it will be taken away.

In verse 19 the introductory particle *kēn* brings the Address to a conclusion. The path (here as *'orḥôth*) denotes a manner of living—though some commentators choose to modify slightly the Hebrew to read 'fate/end', i.e., of the one who is 'greedy for material gain' (*bōṣea' beṣa'*). The root word here refers to 'bringing something to an end, cutting off', or a second sense of gaining something by violent means, suggesting that rather than a root with two meanings, we are looking at a homograph. (And as an aside, I would say that non-native speakers or readers should be far more reluctant about modifying any language that is not their own, unless there is overwhelming evidence for doing so; modifying a foreign language usually leads to arbitrary readings that suit the modifier's agenda.) It is conceivable that there is a chiasm in vv. 17-19 using the unusual terms *ba'al kānāph* for 'the bird' (v. 17), their lives (*naphšōthām*) in v. 18, and *nepheš b^{e} 'alāyw* describing those who are masters of their own lives.

1.20-33 Wisdom Herself Speaks

Wisdom shouts in the street; in the squares she raises her voice.
At the head of the busy street corner she calls, at the entrance of the city gates she speaks out.
'<u>How long</u> will you simple ones love being simple, (how long will) you who scoff enjoy scoffing, and you fools despise knowledge?
Heed my rebuke! Let me speak my mind to you, let me reveal my words to you!
<u>Because</u> you refused my call and none paid heed when I stretched out my hand (to help you),
And <u>because</u> you have ignored all my advice and would not accept my reproof.
<u>So</u> I shall laugh when you meet calamity, and mock when panic overtakes you.

When panic comes like a disaster and calamity comes like a whirlwind and trouble and distress overtake you.
Then they may call me, but I won't answer, they may urgently seek me, but won't find me,
Because they hated knowledge and chose not to fear the Lord,
They did not accept my advice and scorned my rebuke.
So let them 'eat of the fruit' of their ways, and let them be satisfied with their own advice,
For apostasy kills the simple-minded, while complacency of the fools destroys them,
But those who listen to me may be secure and may live in safety, dreading nothing'.

The section is a well-formed piece of writing, dividing into four parts—1.20-21, 22-27, 28-31, 32-33. Changes in the pronouns used suggest this structured division.

Beginning in 1.20-21 we meet Lady Wisdom calling out her warnings in public spaces. Four roughly parallel colons with four verbal imperfectives that stress her constant or frequent calls identify major town spaces as she calls to the public to hear and heed what she has to say. The reference is all third person singular, so it objectively describes personified Wisdom herself and her actions. The personification of Wisdom may be unique to Israel; it is certainly not to be found in Chinese Wisdom.

Wisdom's speech in vv. 22-27 is then quoted and one notes that it changes the form of address to second person as Lady Wisdom speaks directly to her audiences, warning of what could happen if they failed to heed her advice. She shows no sympathy for any who fail to attend, and subsequently experience disaster. Presumably her audiences are the younger generations, but not necessarily so.

At vv. 28-31 those addressed are spoken of in the third person plural, stating that she will mock all those who inevitably suffer as a result of acting foolishly, despising her advice. See also below re language use in vv. 28-30.

Verses 32-33 conclude her initial speech using the contrast of what will 'kill' and what will promote living in security.

It has been suggested, based on an analysis of contents, that the section vv. 20-33 is constructed in a generally chiastic form (Trible, 1975). However, while there is clearly a rhetorical chiasm in vv. 26-27 with 'calamity–panic-panic-calamity' providing a focus for the unit, beyond that the chiasm becomes more speculative, for the reference to 'my counsel' ('*ᵃṣāthî*) in v. 25 and v. 30 and the references to the 'simple' and 'foolish' in v. 30 along with 'reproof', though present, do not constitute a strict chiasm.

Whether this section was a piece originating in an independent source is a question some have asked given that its topic is new and its perspective and literary context very different from the preceding 1.2-7 and 8-19. However, other references to Lady Wisdom and the contrast between her and the 'Loose' Woman, suggest strongly that there was an established tradition within Israelite Wisdom of using the feminine *ḥokmāh* as a strategic educational model. Here in Proverbs there are several examples, including the final chapter, 31.10-31, that speak to this. Even if one could prove that these sections were originally independent units now integrated into the present text, it nevertheless would remain as one of the many literary forms within the Wisdom 'toolkit', and as such enhances the overall purpose of this collection of sayings.

In terms of the language used in this speech, it is to be noted that in vv. 28-30 Wisdom speaks in a manner that is also used elsewhere of Yahweh speeches (Hos. 5.6), but there is a distinction in that Yahweh speeches use first and second person speech—'I/you'—whereas here it is 'I/me/my/they'. In other words, Wisdom recognizes her subordinate status and is speaking on her own cognizance.

1.20-21 Lady Wisdom is introduced, though the term 'wisdom' (fem. sg.) is given as a plural *ḥokmôth*, the significance of which, if any, is elusive and it occurs so rarely—three of its four occurrences are in this book, see also 9.1 and 24.7. That the verbs associated with it are all singular settles the problem for the interpreter. Wisdom as a woman is also featured in 3.13-18; 4.6-9; 7.4; 8.1-3; 9.1-6, as well as in the closing ch. 31.

The picture drawn is of Lady Wisdom calling out in the various public outdoor spaces found in an ancient city, in its alleyways, squares, street corners, and importantly, the 'gates' in the walled city, the rooms set into the entrance gateway where the more official business of a town was conducted. The presentation is intended to heighten the importance of Wisdom's call to all in the community, with the imperfect verbs hinting at frequency or to her on-going call activity. There is also a sense that her call is energetic and urgent in the use of the root *rnn* that normally suggests shouting. This is an unusual but very effective example of personification. As a general statement, four roughly parallel colons draw a comprehensive picture, serving as an introduction to her 'speech' as reported in vv. 22-27.

1.22-27 Directing her speech to a wide audience, Lady Wisdom expresses frustration at the slowness with which people are responding to her reproof (*tôkaḥath*). Inevitably, first person speech dominates her presentation. The opening *'ad māthay*, so typical of the Hebrew Lament literature (e.g., Pss. 74.10; 82.2; Hab. 1.2), serves all three elements in her complaint (v. 22). It implies that this audience has not yet responded to her admonitions. She addresses them as 'simple ones' (*pᵉtāyîm*), 'scoffers' (*lēṣîm*), and 'fools' (*kᵉsîlîm*), terms guaranteed to challenge her audiences.

In v. 23 we note a call to 'turn back', or in this context 'change your ways' (*tāšûbû*) with respect to 'my reproof' (*lᵉtôkaḥtî*). Wisdom here is most active, making numerous attempts to persuade the simple and foolish to amend their ways, which, if they fail to change, will inevitably lead to disaster (vv. 26-27). Wisdom calls for them to heed the words spoken and such help as is on offer (v. 24), warning that when trouble arrives, belated calls for Wisdom's help will result only in her mocking laughter. The context is that of threats or warnings that, if heeded, might deter negative outcomes.

What in Hebrew is literally *Let my spirit bubble up its thoughts to you* is a fascinating expression in that the Hebrew verb used refers to something flowing or bubbling up, that when applied metaphorically pictures a kind of non-stop activity. What is bubbling up here is portrayed as *rûḥî*, generally rendered in translations as 'my spirit'. I regard the verb as volitional with the noun *rûaḥ* describing what Wisdom wishes to convey to the reader. But what is this 'spirit'? What might result from Wisdom's 'bubbling up'? The context suggests some form of advice or counsel, but the use of *rûḥî* seems to imply something far more profound than mere talk, though that is the word used in the parallel colon. Together I read the two clauses as emphasizing what Wisdom wishes to say, something like '*I want to* <u>*make myself and my words*</u> *perfectly clear…*'(?). I understand that *rûaḥ* may not have an equivalent noun in English, though the dictionaries make various suggestions for contextual possibilities—'wind, breath, spirit, odour'. I am suggesting that it speaks of that which is real and relatable but invisible, intangible, ethereal, mysterious, something potently active, a force or energy of some kind, so have chosen the 'self' notion as its intended sense here.

Verse 24 points back to Wisdom's preceding attempts to have people listen to her: 'I called…, you refused/rejected…, I offered my hand, but there was no response'. It leads then into Wisdom's reaction (vv. 25-33). 'Since you have ignored my every advice, accepted none of my reproof, so I will laugh and mock…'. When Lady Wisdom is scorned, she is no longer polite! She threatens to laugh when inevitable disaster befalls those who fail to heed her advice. On two occasions in this section, v. 25 and v. 30, the noun *ʿᵃṣāthî*, 'advice/counsel', is used. This noun can be described as defining the task of the 'professional' Sage, giving advice (see Jer. 18.18). Here it functions also as an inclusio for the section.

Verses 26-27 present as a chiasm, meaning that readers' attention is drawn to the themes of 'calamity' (*'ēd*) and 'panic' (*paḥad*), the certainty of disaster or troubles occurring and the desperate panicked response to same. The reality of human experience is that all encounter both the joys and the disappointments of daily life. Lady Wisdom is reminding her recalcitrant audience that if her advice is not heeded, then when those times of stress and trouble loom and she receives their belated appeals for rescue, she will not be of any positive help, in fact she will simply mock them.

Her response is outlined in vv. 28-29. When trouble (*ṣārāh wᵉṣûqāh*) arrives, as it inevitably will, and people call to her for help, she will not answer, they will look for her but not find her. And the simple reason for her reaction is that people have shown contempt for 'knowledge' and did not prioritize 'the fear of the Lord.' The use of the verb 'call' (*qr'*) here echoes that of Wisdom's 'call' in v. 20, but in this case their call will not be answered, they may seek but will not find, both common warning motifs.

Verse 30 offers an explanation for this lack of response similar to that in v. 25, while in v. 31 it is expressed more pictorially using the metaphor of eating 'the fruit (*pᵉrî*) of their own ways', the 'produce' of their manner of living. Just as they ate their fill of normal food, so would they eat their fill of the consequences of their refusal to attend to Wisdom's advice. Wisdom thus challenges the scoffers and fools to face reality and accept her advice.

The closing two verses, vv. 32-33, are added in justification of, or encouragement to listen to Wisdom because there is a choice to be made—to be 'killed' or to 'live without the fear of disaster'. This life-and-death model provides an example of Wisdom literature's simplification of reality, following the same approach as does Deuteronomy. Heeding Wisdom's advice should have its reward, hope for a pleasant life free from cares and troubles, though it cannot be guaranteed; failure to heed its advice is to act unwisely and thus cause diminution of one's life. The noun chosen to refer to a safe and secure life is *beṭaḥ*, the root conveying a sense of trust and faithfulness, thus an 'assured' life.

PROVERBS 2

2.1-22 Second Address

This Second Address is complex and its contents rather repetitive. That it represents an editor's rough compilation of similar ideas is a possible explanation, but it is certainly not a carefully argued literary piece. After the initial 'My child…' the *Voice* raises four potential conditions ('if…' *'im*) in *vv.* 1-4 followed by an apodosis ('then…,' *'āz*) in v. 5, with an explanation ('for…' *kî*) attached in vv. 6-8. A second apodosis ('then…,' *'āz*) begins v. 9, with ('for…' *kî*) vv. 10-11 offering an explanation using four separate wisdom terms. A series of participles in vv. 12-15 describes those whom wisdom can rescue, then vv. 16-19 describe the 'other woman' (*'iššāh zārāh*) and the 'way of death' she represents. Finally in vv. 20-22 the *Voice* justifies its advice as offering a happier future. While several references to 'wisdom' are to be expected, one feature of these verses is the frequent use of the two nouns 'path' (*'orḥôth*) and 'way' (*derek*) throughout vv. 8-20, a reminder that wisdom is a matter of practice, not theory or mere information.

For this reader the chapter divides into three sections as follows: 2.1-15, 16-19, 20-22. There is a close connection between the first and second sections with the comment about wisdom 'saving' one from the way of evil (*l^{e}haṣṣil^{e}kā min*…, v. 12) being taken up in the second section, the beginning of v. 16 featuring the same *l^{e}haṣṣil^{e}kā min*…, 'to deliver you from…', here delivering from the 'outsider' woman.

2.1-15

My child, If you accept my words, and (if) my commandments you treasure within you,
Having your ears attentive to wisdom, inclining your heart/mind to understanding,
Indeed, if you call out for insight and cry out for understanding,

> *If you seek after it like (you seek) silver, and like hidden treasures go in search of it,*
> *Then you may come to understand what it is to fear the Lord, to find the knowledge of God.*
> *For/Indeed the Lord gives wisdom and from his mouth comes knowledge and understanding*
> *He lays up sound wisdom for those who are upright, a shield to those who walk blamelessly,*
> *To guard the paths of justice and protect the paths of the faithful.*
> *Then you may understand righteousness and justice, and from the upright ones every good pathway.*
> *For/Indeed let wisdom be in your heart/mind, and may knowledge please your being.*
> *May prudence protect (watch over) you and understanding guard you,*
> *To deliver you from the evil ones, from the one speaking of perversions,*
> *(From) those who abandon the paths of uprightness to walk in the ways of darkness,*
> *Who rejoice in doing evil, who delight in deceitfulness of evil,*
> *Whose paths are crooked, and devious in their ways.*

2.1-4 The initial sub-set of conditionals presents a series of possible actions, followed by a pair of potential positive outcomes that focus on understanding '*the fear of the Lord*' and finding '*the knowledge (of God)*', thus echoing the basic notions expressed in 1.7 but here contrasting with their being despised by scoffers in 1.29.

The *Voice* speaks of possibilities: If one accepts Wisdom's words, if one treasures her commandments, if one has an *ear* attentive to wisdom, if one inclines the *heart* to understanding, if one cries out for insight, calls out for understanding, if one seeks it like one desperate to find treasure (vv. 1-4), then…! ***2.5-8, 9-11.*** These two sub-units that complete the conditionals in vv. 1-4 offer closely parallel texts and overlapping content. Both v. 5 and v. 9 begin with the phrase *'āz tābîn*, 'then you may understand…', marking the two apodoses, the potential results of the preceding conditions, followed by *kî*, 'for…', that explains the result or consequence. Both units focus on the gift of 'understanding' such that it makes the point that (a) 'fear of the Lord' and (b) 'knowledge of God' in the first example equate with (c) 'righteousness, justice and equity' and (d) 'every good path' in the second. All four elements are complementary and together define Wisdom. There is probably no more complete statement of the role of Wisdom in Israel's communal and religious life than is given here. The suggestion that Wisdom in Israel was 'secular', and thus of less importance theologically, has been a feature of some modern scholarship.

Such a valuation is not that of ancient Israel but rather derives from a western mindset, a misreading of ancient Israel's worldview.

2.5-8 Then… (v. 5). The emphasis is obviously on a commitment to seeking both to obtain, and then to live with, Wisdom as one's primary guide. If these conditions are met, then a positive outcome may ensue—one should gain an understanding of what it is to 'fear the Lord', and at the same time discover (*māṣāʾ*) 'knowledge of God'. These two intimately connected and mutually defining expressions summarize the gift that is Lady Wisdom herself. However, as explained above, the Sage could never guarantee the positive outcome of any particular lifestyle, so rendering the verbs in a manner that appears to assure such an outcome is problematic. The claims would have to be understood as hyperbole, or as deliberate emphasis seeking to convince the younger generation to accept and live by its counsel; only by living according to Wisdom's advice can one come to discover its true worth.

Verse 6 begins with the marker *kî*, 'for…', to introduce the reason or basis for the preceding assurance—that Wisdom is a gift (*yittēn*) from the Lord; knowledge and understanding, even if limited, proceed from Yahweh in Israel's worldview, attributing the Sage's insight to a divine source—hence the verb 'discover'. It is here that one can note a difference between Israelite Wisdom and that of Confucius, for the latter does not place Wisdom in a 'religious' context; rather, it is of purely human origin, a path (道) of choice attainable by living out the core values (德) as defined. 'To live in the company of Great Man is the finest thing possible. How can a man be considered wise if…he does not live in such surroundings?' (里仁爲美。擇不出仁， 焉得知？)

The notion of the Lord 'storing up' wisdom in v. 7 for any who are 'upright' is taken to mean that he will provide wisdom in abundance. Rather than the traditional or more general *ḥokmāh*, the noun used here is *tûšiyyāh*, a rare term generally restricted to the Wisdom material. Its root is *yšh*, and BDB suggests 'sound wisdom' as a meaning. NRSV follows, but JPS suggests 'ability', with others also seeing it as a reference to a practical skill—see the taxonomic issue noted above re. 1.2-7. It clearly refers to something positive and advantageous. As a gift for those considered 'upright', it appears as a reward. Its additional function is as a protective 'shield' for those whose 'walk' or manner of life is blameless (*tōm*), i.e., a life lived with integrity.

In 2.8 that blameless lifestyle is further described in terms of 'justice' and 'faithfulness'. These two notions are fundamental to the Israelite view of what it was to be 'upright' in every aspect of one's community involvement. 'Faithfulness' (*ḥesed*) has religious as well as a more everyday sense of one who can be trusted—God's faithfulness, as well as faithful human relationships. For Confucius these attributes (德) are also basic though not linked in any way with a religious worldview.

2.9-11 *'Then you may understand…,'* introduces a second list of the consequences of the conditionals in 2.1-4, the *kî* particle beginning the explanatory note and repeating much of the content of vv. 5-8. It is conceivable that these verses are an alternative version of the material in 2.5-8.

Verse 11 uses the verbs *nṣr*, 'guard', and *šmr*, 'keep/protect', as does v. 8, using them here in reverse order. The noun *ma'gāl*, a path or well-worn track, introduces a third term for one's manner of living and here described as marked by 'goodness'. Four terms are used—wisdom, knowledge, prudence and understanding—to speak of Wisdom's contribution to one's enhanced life.

The reference to 'heart' and 'soul' (NRSV) in v. 10 links together two elements that encapsulate the very core of one's being. 'Heart' (*lēb*) can refer also to the mind, to rationality, one's decision-making ability, and the *nepheš* represents the inner being, the life-force (see Gen. 2.7).

2.12-15 Verse 12 begins with an infinitive *lehaṣṣîlekā min…*, repeated in v. 16, that points to the purpose of wisdom being that of 'rescuing' from *derek ra'*, the 'way of evil'. It is explained in more detail as one being protected 'from those who…' (a) speak perversely; (b) forsake the 'upright' path; (c) walk in darkness; (d) rejoice in doing evil; (e) delight in perverseness; (f) whose paths are crooked; and (g) those whose ways are devious. This group of participles shows again how Wisdom's assistance is very practical, saving one from taking the wrong path. In the Confucian context the figure of paths and crooked ways is a shared concept for a way of life: 'If you will appoint upright persons to the places now held by the crooked, you will be making the crooked straight' (子曰：擧値錯諸枉，能使枉者値)

A feature of these several verses and the following sub-unit is the use of repetition: *tahpukôth* (vv. 12, 14), *'orḥôth* (vv. 13, 15), *ra'* (vv. 12, 14). The *tahpukôth* are words or speech intended to 'overthrow' (*ḥpk*), to dissuade, always negative in its intent.

2.16-19

May you be rescued from the 'outsider' woman, from the alien woman and her smooth talk,
Who abandons the partner of her youth and dismisses the covenant with her God.
For her house(?) sinks to Death and her pathways to the Shades.
None who go to her return, nor do they find a way back to 'life'.

The focus of the unit is entirely given over to a warning about Wisdom's role in helping one to avoid becoming involved in problematic sexual relationships. I have expressed it as a volitional, and used present tense verbs to capture the permanent threat or challenge that such a wily woman can and does pose.

Here again the 'rescue' theme is repeated following the infinitive *l^e^haṣṣîl^e^kā min…* form in v. 12, this time with a certain kind of woman as its object. The woman in question is generic, described as *'iššāh zārāh*, literally a 'strange/foreign' woman, also identified as *nokriyyāh*, literally 'foreigner (woman)'. The two adjectives are presumably derogatory, jargon terms for any 'outsider' woman, with the implication that her morals were in doubt, even if there was no substance to the aspersion. JPS suggests 'forbidden woman', a less judgmental identification. The most basic sense of both adjectives relates to difference in the broad sense, whether it be that of belonging to another family, another tribe or nation, not to actual morality, hence '*loose*' woman (NRSV) is far from an adequate representation. Given that within ancient Israelite families it was absolutely permissible for a man to have a sexual relationship with females other than his wife or wives—take Abraham as one example (Gen. 16)—the issue here is not primarily to do with immorality, but is that of sex *outside the family-sanctioned setting*. The note about the 'house' in v. 18 lends support to this perspective. Israelites saw themselves as God's specially-chosen people; everyone other than their own community or family could be described as *zār*, or a *nēker*. 'Outsiders' of all stripes, from family to tribe to nation, could be described by these two adjectives—see Deut. 25.5. Here in this context, we are looking specifically at sexual relationships outside the family or family-sanctioned arrangements.

2.17 describes the woman as, (a) one who has abandoned the friend she had during her younger days (*'allûph n^e^ 'ûreyhā*), and (b) one who 'forgot' i.e., deliberately dismissed, the covenant with 'her God/god' (*'^e^lōheyhā*). As for the initial phrase, the root *n'r* usually refers to one who is quite young, though there are some exceptions. Some commentators see this as a reference to her husband (see also BDB), but there is no reason to make that assumption if the phrase actually means ‘a young companion’ regardless of gender. If this is the case then the issue is her fidelity, her trustworthiness, not her sexual conduct. The second condemnatory phrase represents a purely religious failure, again not immorality. Furthermore, it is not possible to know whether the covenant reference is a reference to Yahweh as Israel’s God and the covenant with Israel, or whether it refers to the woman’s foreign gods, but this latter relationship is not usually spoken of using ‘covenantal’ language.

2.18 begins the explanation, the grounds for the advice being offered. The initial *kî* can be read as an emphatic, ‘Indeed’, but here more likely to be ‘For/Because…’. Using the language of generalization, the *Voice* argues that associating with a woman like her can only have one outcome—‘death’. The Hebrew text is problematic in that it reads literally as ‘for (it) sinks down (*šāḥâ*) to death her house’ with the verb as feminine while ‘house’ is masculine. Repointing the text—reading a noun *shûḥâ*, ‘pit’, instead of *shāhāh*—may resolve the syntax issue as it then forms a clearer parallel to the following ‘shades’, but even without the arbitrary emendation its point is obvious, namely that one who ‘goes down’ to her house/family is heading for ‘death’, used metaphorically as in 7.27. The noun *r^e^phā’îm* in the second half verse is interesting as possibly related to the verb ‘sink’, but also meaning ‘ghosts’ (Job 26.5) or ‘giants’ (Josh. 17.15), clearly connected to mythical figures and death. The noun *ma‘gāl* in vv. 9, 12 reappears here to describe one’s ‘path’ or manner of living.

In v. 19 the final fate is sealed—there is no way back (*lō’ y^e^šûbûn*) once the path of the ‘non-family woman’ is followed. Again, one notes the generalized language used in an attempt to make plain the danger that one confronts if choosing to listen to the woman’s words. The statement sets out a belief among the Sages with regard to the impact that such a woman has, a life-long impact. It is the plural noun *ḥayyîm*, an abstract plural, that has a broad sense of not just ‘life’ in its physical expression for it also relates to the quality of one’s living, one’s experience of the best that life offers. Its antonym, ‘death’ or *môt*, likewise refers to the deadly or deadening manner in which one passes through this life until physical death becomes a reality.

2.20-22

> *Therefore, you should walk in the way of the good ones, keeping to the paths of the just persons,*
> *Indeed, may the upright dwell in the land, and the innocent may they be left to remain in it.*
> *But let the wicked be cut off from the land, and may those who are treacherous be uprooted from it.*

Continuing the metaphor of a path and a manner of walking, the *Voice* urges the audience to follow the example set by the good and the righteous, the upright and innocent, echoing thoughts from 2.8.

The *kî* with which v. 21 begins could be the asseverative ‘Indeed…’, adding force to the advice, or simply be the explanatory ‘Because…’ that underlines the prospect of remaining in the land. The assumption is that the noun *'ereṣ*, here without the definite article, refers to the Promised Land. The theme of living and holding onto possession of the land as promised is a basic idea in Deuteronomy—obedience to Torah will guarantee continued occupation and never being driven from the land (see Deut. 28.58-63). Here that background emerges and is expressed in an unusual application of the root *ytr*, normally referring to those who remain or are left behind, a portion of an original group. The form here is a passive imperfect *yiwwāth*^{e}*rû* indicating being allowed to remain in place.

In contrast to v. 21, v. 22 speaks of those who will be ‘cut off’ (*krt*), a commonly-used expression in Deuteronomic language describing one’s fate or punishment. It is paralleled by the verb ‘uproot’, a metaphor for complete removal from the soil, one’s *terroir*. In these contrasts Wisdom’s alternatives are set forth—the hope that the young will hear and respond to the advice offered and reap its potential benefits over against the fate imagined for all those who reject it.

Proverbs 3

3.1-12 Third Address

My child, do not neglect my teaching, may your mind hold firm my commandments.
Indeed, may they provide for you length of days and years of life and an increase in wellbeing.
Do not allow loyalty or faithfulness desert you, bind them around your neck, inscribe them on the tablet of your heart.
So may you discover favour and approval in the sight of (both) God/gods and humanity.
Trust in the Lord with all your heart, and do not depend on your own insight.
In all your ways acknowledge him and may he make straight your pathways.
Do not become a self-appointed wise person, fear the Lord and turn away from evil.
Let it be for your physical healing, and refreshment for your bones.
Give honour to the Lord from your substance, and from the firstfruits of all your produce.
May your storehouses be filled with plenty and your wine vats overflow with wine.
Do not despise, my child, the Lord's discipline, and do not grow weary of his reproof,
For the one whom the Lord loves he reproves, and like a father (reproves) the child in whom he delights.

Like the Second Address in 2.1, this address begins with the *Voice* speaking to a younger person. Conditional forms dominated the Second Address, while here it is negative imperatives (3.1, 3, 5, 7, 11) that give the collection a distinctive tone and identity—they warn against actions that would prove harmful, while assuring what could or might result from heeding the advice given. Again, the point is that these latter are not promises, for the sages knew that assured outcomes were impossible to determine, but they represent potential outcomes, *inducements* to follow the advice offered.

In terms of the overall structure, this reader suggests a five-part division, vv. 1-2, 3-4, 5-6, 7-10, 11-12. Not every section is of equal length. The basis of this division is that each section begins with or contains a negative command, then adds positive commands and concludes with an imperfect verb(s) that suggests a potential outcome.

While the first two sub-sections, 3.1-2, 3-4 focus on Wisdom itself, the following sub-sections, 3.5-6, 7-10, 11-12, are commands and exhortations centred around one's relationship with the Lord.

3.1-2 As was the case in 1.8, the noun *torah* has a general meaning of 'teaching/instruction' rather than the narrower sense of 'the Law'; it is advice from the *Voice* rather than a divine command. The imperative uses the verb *šākaḥ*, 'forget', that is often used to express a wilful forgetting, a deliberate rejection of an idea or allegiance. The command 'not to forget' is then balanced by a positive call, in which the verb *yṣr* requires giving close and conscious attention to 'my commandments', with the 'heart' or mind as the repository (see 2.2, 10). The use of the term 'commandments' (*mišpāṭ*) should be understood to be one of several Wisdom terms for its own advice (see 2.1; 4.4), not confined to legislation.

Verse 2 begins with the *kî* particle, usually explanatory, but here also possibly as the emphatic particle, 'Indeed/Truly…'. What the *Voice* suggests is that a 'long life'—literally 'extension of days and years of lives', a nominal phrase—marked by increased personal well-being (*šālôm*) may come to one who heeds the counsel offered. These two terms summarize the ideal life—increased longevity and welfare, ideals frequently noted and prized.

For Confucius also, 'Man's life span depends on his uprightness. He who goes on living without it escapes disaster only by good fortune' (人之生也直，罔之生也幸而免).

3.3-4 A second negative command demands that two significant values—*ḥesed wᵉ'emeth*, 'loyalty and faithfulness/truth'—not be abandoned. The double expression is a significant Hebrew phrase relating to the underpinning values that maintain personal relationships (Gen. 24.49; Exod. 34.6; Deut. 7.9; Ps. 25.10). The form of the command here seems a little unusual in that it requires the individual to 'not let <u>them</u> forsake <u>you</u>', rather than saying, '<u>You</u> must not abandon <u>them</u>'. It is followed by more active verbs in the calls to 'bind them…, write them…' metaphorically on one's person. Tying them around one's neck suggests an item worn externally like an amulet in which the object or contents serve as a constant physical reminder of how to live. Writing them on the ‘tablet (*lûaḥ*) of one’s heart’ suggests a conscious intention to abide by the commands.

If these orders are followed, then one may find *ḥēn*, ‘favour/kindness’, along with *śēkel-ṭôb*, ‘good approval’ in the eyes both of God and of one’s fellow citizens.

In Confucian terms: ‘Let your speech be loyal and trustworthy; your actions sincere and respectful’ (言忠信，行篤敬，雖蠻貘之邦行矣)。

3.5-6 The first two calls in 3.1-2, 3-4 follow the same pattern, opening the case with a negative imperative. Here in vv. 5-6, by contrast, a positive call begins, then followed by the negative command and a further positive call, with an incentive added to close.

The opening call in v. 5 is for complete trust in (*b*^{e}*taḥ ’el*) the Lord, a hearty commitment to rely on him. This is then expressed in the reverse form, a negative command not to rely on one’s own understanding. The use of a contrasting pair is a typical Wisdom form of instruction, but it is not a matter of A ruling out B; it is not intending to undermine or diminish the use of one’s intellect or reflective powers. What the saying does in fact do is it establishes priorities. Given that Wisdom sets dependence upon the Lord as the gold standard, that is what should be prioritized, with personal ideas subject to dependence on the Lord. But what does it mean to ‘trust in the Lord’ in this Wisdom context? It can only mean to follow Wisdom’s instruction and advice, as noted in the definition in 1.7.

Verse 6 calls for one to ‘acknowledge’ (*dā‘ēhû*) the Lord as one walks the way/path through life; it explains the values of v. 5. The verb ‘know’ speaks of intimate relationship (Gen. 4.1), so it is calling for that state of mind in which one is always conscious of what the Lord’s requirements are, such as love, justice, trustworthiness—in fact, it is to reflect the divine nature in one’s own daily walk.

It closes with the express wish that one’s path through life might be ‘straight’, *yāšār* being an adjective that describes something smooth as well as ethically upright. I understand the verb to be volitional, expecting that the Lord would honour the relationship in which he is so acknowledged.

3.7-10 This longer sub-section has two parts: (a) begins with a negative command followed by a double positive call and an expressed hope for personal benefit (vv. 7-8), then (b) a further encouragement that links honouring the Lord in cultic terms with the expectation that it will prove to be of much material benefit (vv. 9-10). Both parts of this sub-section relate to the Deuteronomic belief that obedience to Torah will bring untold blessings, as outlined in Deut. 7.12-14. However, for the Sage there is always the caveat that one cannot guarantee such a positive outcome; it can only be hoped for.

Opening sub-section (a) is the call, 'Do not be wise in your own eyes!' The sense is clearly a warning not to consider one's own version of what is wise to be the acceptable standard. Why? Because there is only one standard, and that is 'to be in awe of Yahweh', *yᵉr'ā 'eth yhwh,* as in 1.7. That 'fear/awe' in practical terms means a deliberate turning aside from evil (*ra'*) of all kinds—the noun is general. If one makes this commitment, then the *Voice* expects, not promises, that it may bring physical or bodily healing and refreshment (3.8). The Hebrew term *šor* rendered 'flesh' is actually a rare term found only here and in Ezek. 16.4 with a basic meaning 'navel'. Parallel to it, the text uses the word 'bones' (*'aṣmôth*), so together they represent the physical body, or whole person.

3.9 demands 'honour' for the Lord. It was to be expressed by means of giving literally 'from (= some of) your substance/wealth'. The phrase *mēhônekā* implies part of one's goods. The second half of the bicolon speaks of the 'first fruits of produce', the offerings made at the annual harvest festival (Lev. 23.15-21), indicating that conforming to cultic demands of the Law (see Exod. 23.19; Num. 28.26-31; Deut. 26.1-15) was a wise thing to do by way of giving honour to the Lord. As such this text is rather unusual, since cultic matters normally were not a concern of the Israelite Sage. In that respect Confucius' advice differs; for him the observance of 'the rites' was crucial if one aspired to qualify as a Great Man (仁者). There is no religious content in this practice, but it calls for honouring (not worshipping!) one's ancestors, showing respectful relationships to maintain community harmony. 'Let youth practice filial duty; let it practice fraternal duty; let it give itself to being reliable' (子曰：弟子入則孝，出則弟，謹而信，汎愛衆，而親仁).

One feature of interest in v. 10 is that it seems to imply that the purpose of conforming to the dictates of the religious Law was to acquire benefits from the Lord rather than it being a conscious act of true piety; it raises the question of motivation in religious activity. Full barns and overflowing vats of wine, and probably olive oil also, were potential benefits to the one who kept the Law, according to Deuteronomic theory. Was the *Voice* appealing to the self-interest of his young students? The advice here certainly does align with Wisdom's earthy practicality, its call for prudence and caution when in certain situations, such as Qoheleth's advice in Eccl. 5.1-6; 8.2-4. When confronted by those in power or in a religious context, one needs to consider carefully how one should best act and react in order to avoid unwanted consequences and to obtain what was being offered.

3.11-12 The Third Address concludes with the theme of divine reproof, and as such is of particular interest because it takes up the problem of the disjuncture between the Deuteronomic thesis of blessings and curses dependent on one's actions, and the reality of innocent suffering or failed rewards. It is a discrete unit that, in terms of content, is thoroughly generalized and has no direct connection to the preceding material.

The Lord's 'discipline', *mûsār*, is here emphasized by the use of the noun *tôkaḥath* and the verb from the same root *ykḥ*. A father's treatment of a favoured child is the analogical basis from which the *Voice* appeals to a young person to accept what is interpreted as the Lord's 'love'; it projects from a human example onto the deity. The verb *'āhab*, 'love', is used in two senses in these chapters of Proverbs, emotional love and physical love; it is used of one's attitude to wisdom and of the Lord's attitude to humans, and it is also used for sexual love-making.

In v. 11 the subject is immediately identified—divine 'discipline'. Two negative imperatives follow as warnings. In v. 12 likewise, the subject is provided first. In terms of syntax, placing the two objects in initial position highlights the two themes: (a) that divine reproof is to be expected, and (b) that it is applied only to those whom the Lord loves. Perhaps the intention is to offer assurance to the young that unexpected disasters, innocent suffering, failed promises and similar are to be welcomed despite the hardships, for they are in fact signs, evidence that one is loved by the Lord. The logic is torturous, but hopefully can be positively skewed. Eliphaz in Job 5.17-18 makes a statement similar to vv. 11-12 in support of the simplistic Deuteronomic thesis (Job 5.20-27), one that Job rejects utterly in chapters 6–7 and all readers of the book know it to be problematic.

The difficulty here is that the nature of the 'discipline' is unstated. There is no suggestion that the Lord's 'discipline' (*mûsār*) is punishment for wrongdoing, so it is left to the reader to make assumptions that all negative experiences and disappointments one encounters in life are (a) initiated by God, and (b) have an educational or positive purpose and goal. As a general statement of a theological principle, it is deeply problematic, and while 'bad things do happen to good people', as also the reverse, such are simply facts in our human experience whether such are attributed to God or not. That 'discipline', so-called, always serves an educational benefit requires one to adopt a particular mindset, a certain theology, so it takes a very mature person to view 'discipline' or 'reproof' in any form as a possible expression of love, especially of God's love, because it sets up a conflict with divine justice.

3.13-18 Praising Wisdom

Happy is the person who has discovered Wisdom, the one who acquires understanding,
For her benefit is better than that of silver and the profit she offers more than that of gold.
She is more precious than rubies, and none of your valuable objects can compare with her.
Length of days lies in her right hand, in her left (hand) are riches and honour.
Her ways are pleasant ways, and all her paths are peaceful.
She is a life-giving tree to those who hold on to her, and all who grasp her are made happy.

Another discrete unit with its own focus has been inserted at this point in the collection. It has no obvious connection to the surrounding material, so it can only be read for its present content. That the unit opens and closes with references to happiness (*'šr*) marks it as special—the use of *'ašrē*, 'happy', links it with a number of Psalms—1.1; 32.1, 2; 41.1 etc.. The *Voice* speaks of Wisdom in the third person, praising her for her incomparable richness, a value that surpasses that of prized materials and jewels, as well as affirming her contribution to one's long and joyous life of *shalom*.

3.13 uses the generic term *'ādām*, humanity, in both half-verses, an unusual feature in itself, in order to make the statement completely universal. The situation envisaged is of one who 'has found' Wisdom, further elaborated as the one who 'acquires' (on-going) understanding; the use of a perfect verb form followed by an imperfect speaks of a continuing process of accessing Wisdom. The reason why the *Voice* could make such a comprehensive statement is in v. 14—the firm belief that the benefit, the return from an investment in Wisdom, is priceless, beyond the value of silver and gold.

Seeking material reward by walking the Wisdom way was never a goal in Confucian Wisdom either; rather, it was simply doing what was expected of one and doing it diligently: 'He who prioritizes the task and forgets about reward may be called Ideal Man' (仁者先難而後獲，可謂仁矣).

Verse 15 adds to that assessment. Wisdom is more precious than rubies (there is some slight issue with the actual item identified, but see 8.11, 'jewels'), so precious, in fact, that no other material of value, no *ḥēpeṣ*, can compare with it. Why suddenly there is a second person reference in this line is unclear.

Long life was always regarded in Israel as a sign of divine blessing (see e.g., 28.16; Ps. 91.16). Here in v. 16 the figurative language uses right and left hands to symbolize being gifted longevity, riches and honour by Wisdom herself, as the results that should arise from following her advice. That these are her 'gifts' is a manner of speaking, whereas it is generally believed that they would derive only from Yahweh. It would be going too far to evaluate longevity as higher than other benefits despite it being offered by the right hand, usually symbolic of honour.

Similarly, Confucius emphasized Wisdom as gifting longevity: 'The wise are active, the benevolent one quiet; the wise find pleasure, the benevolent find long life.' (知者動，仁者靜，智者樂，仁者壽).

In v. 17 there is a return to the 'way' and 'path' analogies, now described here as 'lovely', that inspire appreciation and provide *šālôm*. What Wisdom can offer a person is a deep sense of calm and wholeness, as well as the more material 'gifts'.

The final verse likens Wisdom to *'ēṣ ḥayyîm*, 'the tree of life', though given the context of grabbing it (*maḥ*^{a}*zîqîm*), and of grasping hold (*tmk*) of it, it may well refer more to a piece of wood, or even a pole (Gen. 40.19). The metaphor is not absolutely clear in terms of how *'ēṣ*, 'wood/tree/ bramble', might serve as a source of happiness. Linking it to the mythical 'tree of life' in Gen. 2.9 seems logical but nevertheless cryptic unless it points to something constantly growing and stable.

3.19-20 Wisdom in Creation

The Lord by (his) wisdom established the earth, by (his) understanding he set up the heavens;
By his knowledge the depths were broken open, and the heavens dropped down their dew.

Another sudden and unexpected change of theme is introduced by this brief, independent, but highly significant theological statement. By placing YHWH at the head of the statement, the *Voice* gives it emphasis—it was Yahweh's wisdom that was the agent of creation. (See also the initial placement of objects in vv. 11-12)

Three terms central to Wisdom are used—*ḥokmāh* 'wisdom', *t*^{e}*bûnāh* 'understanding', and *da'at* 'knowledge'. It speaks of them being the three vehicles by which it is claimed that Yahweh established the created order, the heavens and the earth. Alternatively, the b^e preposition could also be read as *'...in (his own) wisdom* established...' the world, placing more emphasis on the Lord's doing rather than on Wisdom's role. How this action might have been accomplished is not elaborated, but it is a clear statement of a core belief, The two verbs used here—*ysd*, 'lay a foundation', and *kwn* describing something set or fixed in place—are terms from the world of physical construction, and are often used together poetically—see Ps. 24.2. The *Voice* is laying claim to the centrality of Wisdom in the divine shaping of the universe.

As an alternative account, this statement complements the Elohistic version of creation in Genesis 1, in which it was the divine spoken word that 'accomplished' creation. It is conceivable that v. 20 hints at the imagery of earth being broken open to allow the waters below the earth to burst forth (Gen. 7), while the heavens, via its windows, allowed dew and rain to water it from above. More will be said on this topic in 8.22-31.

3.21-35 Fourth Address

My child, do not let them escape from your vision, guard sound wisdom and prudence,
May they be life(giving) for your inner being and grace for your neck.
Then may you walk safely on your way and your foot never stumble.
If/whenever you lie down you need not fear, and (when) you lie down (may) your sleep be sweet.
Do not fear sudden panic or the storm that overcomes the wicked,
For let the Lord be your confidence(?) and may he preserve your foot from being caught.
Do not refuse the good from one's masters(?) when it is in your power to do so.
Do not order your neighbour to go and return, tomorrow I will give it when it is (there) with you.
Do not plan to do harm against your neighbour when he is living trustingly beside you,
Do not argue with anyone unjustifiably if no harm has been done to you.
Do not envy one who is violent, and do not choose any of his ways.
For the one who is perverse is an abomination to the Lord while the upright are his confidence.
The Lord's curse is on the house of the wicked, but he blesses the dwelling of the righteous
With those who scorn (others) he is scornful, but with the humble he shows grace/favour.
The wise may they inherit honour, but stubborn fools (inherit) disgrace.

The most obvious feature of this Address, apart from its introductory 'My child', is its gathered negative commands each using *'al* with a jussive verb. The two initial qualities that are advocated provide the context for the entire unit—sound wisdom (*tûšiyyāh*) and prudence (*m^e^zimmāh*). The *Voice* calls for these personal qualities never to be forgotten, to have them always in the mind's 'eye'.

The varied contents of the section give the general impression that it represents a collection of disparate commands, with supplementary advice that coheres around several themes—walking/feet/ways (vv. 23, 26), neighbourliness (vv. 28, 29), and the nature of Israel's God (vv. 26, 32-35). It is difficult to determine a clear structure for the section, though a general four-part division seems possible: (a) vv. 21-24 do have the air of an Introduction with v. 21 as the main statement; (b) vv. 22-24 build on it, drawing out potential benefits to any who would receive and conform with the advice; (c) collected negative warnings follow in vv. 25-31 presenting the most basic advice probably directed at a very young audience, with (d) vv. 32-35 justifying the advice based on Yahweh's perceived nature and attitude to both those who do and those who do not live by the call given in the initial v. 21.

3.21-24 The introductory 'My child' points to this section as Instructions. It calls for the young person to establish a strong habit—to guard against (*nzr*) losing sight of something important, i.e., to always be observant of something; that something then is defined as *sound wisdom* and *prudence* (see also 1.4; 2.7). While the sentence structure is unusual with the verb's two objects delayed and placed at the end of the verse, it is a pattern that serves to highlight them in a manner rarely seen. The section as a whole should be read in light of these two highlighted qualities. The two initial qualities in v. 21 are further explained as resulting in one's life being steady and safe, using the 'walk', 'way' and 'foot' metaphors that are now common in this text. Wisdom's potential gift, its advice when followed, promises to enhance one's experience of daily life.

The *Voice* urges attention to both objectives because it is believed that to do so can 'become life' (*yihyû ḥayyîm*) for one's *nephesh*, one's very being (命). The existential verb in the imperfect suggests something on-going, a continuous state of being. The Hebrew plural noun *ḥayyîm* implies a lifetime, good advice for the young starting out in life. The noun *nepheš*, sometimes rendered as 'soul' or 'spirit', is the term used in Gen. 2.7 to describe *'ādām* when animated by God's breath. Whether these English renderings can adequately represent ancient Israel's concept of *nephesh* is debatable, but 'soul' may be too modern and culturally inappropriate to apply here. What one can say is that the advice, when heeded, is assumed to have great benefit for one's experience of what life is and can offer.

The metaphor of grace or graciousness (*ḥēn*) as an adornment for the neck in v. 22 is less clear, though the idea that one's 'sound wisdom' and 'prudence' should be on show like a piece of jewelry around one's neck, does seem to be what is intended.

3.24 begins with a conditional marker *'im*, 'if', here with the wider sense of 'whenever…' with the imperfect verb carrying its frequentative nuance. The verb in question, *šākab*, appears in both halves of this verse and as such is unusual; normally a parallel verb would be used in the second half verse, so some commentators have looked to emending one or the other occurrence, an all-too-common a practice. There is no supporting evidence for emendation here. The verb's basic sense is 'lie down', with the nature of the act defined by other contextual information. The claim is that a life that prioritizes the two qualities mentioned may relieve one of fear (of what? see v. 25) and allow one to go to bed and sleep peacefully.

3.25-26 These two verses pick up the theme of 'fear'—here *'al tîr'ā*—from v. 24, repeating the root word *paḥad* identified as the 'dread' that might suddenly overcome one. Following the previous verse 24, however, this assurance should not have been necessary, hence the hint that these pieces of advice are simply gathered together because of their common association. The 'dread' is then expanded as a metaphorical 'storm' striking the evildoer, similar to the warning to the foolish in 1.26-27. Whether the 'dread' is physical or psychological harm is not clear.

Verse 26 has two significant components: the initial subject word is YHWH. Normally, placing the subject before the verb would imply an emphatic purpose, that it is Yahweh who instils confidence, not some other; the verb is followed by a phrase *bᵉkisleḵā* from the noun *kesel* that usually means 'stupidity'. It cannot possibly carry that sense here, but its use in Job 8.14 and 31.24 shows another sense, namely 'confidence', and it may also refer to part of the human body. Such disparate meanings attested for the root letters clearly indicates that we are dealing with a homograph—only context indicates which meaning should be attributed. The use in Job obviously supports the interpretation adopted above.

The basis of confidence for the *Voice* is that Yahweh is the one to provide it and ensure (*šāmar*) that one's foot did not slip or cause one to stumble, another well-used figure of speech implying failure—see v. 23; 4.12, 27; 5.5; 7.11.

3.27-31 A further five negative commands characterize this section. The calls focus on what not to do in one's personal relationships with 'the neighbour'—one should not fail to do good where possible, nor delay repayments, nor seek to harm, nor quarrel. The fifth call is for one to beware of emulating the neighbour who is violent.

Defining 'neighbour' in this setting has to be very general. When relating to more permanent and settled villages and towns or to more nomadic contexts, the neighbour may be a close relative, or of a more mixed background.

The impression given in this sub-section is of a range of quite separate instructions, perhaps listing core elements in a course designed to teach very young, inexperienced and unsophisticated youths what were some of the most basic attitudes and actions required for life in the community. No motive or justification is given for so acting as each is a simple statement of what has to happen for good neighbourly relationships to be maintained.

In v. 27 the advice is to not withhold 'good' from *bᵉ'ālāyw*, literally 'his/one's masters'. If, as suggested, this is an element in a basic training course, then 'master' is a possible generic term for those with authority in the community. The singular adjective/noun 'good' (*ṭôb*) appears to refer to material goods or good things, but could also conceivably be good deeds. By refusing to act towards a 'superior'(?) who is owed something, be it respect or a material good, one is actually working against that person. Only a fool would refuse to do good when in a position to do as society required. It is as though this is a warning against being stubborn and hard to get along with, impolitic. The idiomatic phrase *bihyôth lᵉ'ēl-yādᵉkā* uses the word *'ēl* with its figurative sense of power, thus referring to one's discretion in the use of one's power or capability.

The call in v. 28 relates to one who is deliberately ornery and difficult, causing the neighbour to wait a day or so, perhaps involving inconvenient travel as well, before returning some item, whether that be a payment or some physical item that had been borrowed. Unneighbourly conduct is inconsiderate and impolite, more the mark of the fool, of one who may be wanting to exert some 'power' over the other for personal satisfaction. No matter what the motive for treating a neighbour so badly, it should never be entertained by any 'upright' member of the community.

The third negative command in v. 29 is to not seek harm against a trusting neighbour. The neighbour's trust is expressed in the phrase *lābetaḥ* as in v. 23. Why would one want to or choose to do harm, especially to one who is living peaceably nearby? What might prompt such a command unless the young person being instructed was known to be or have anti-social or worse tendencies? No motive is offered for the command, no law is cited, just a blanket prohibition based on what the Sage tradition considers the only 'right' thing to do. The verb used in this prohibition is *ḥrš* whose basic meaning has to do with incising marks on a surface with some kind of tool, so its figurative use implies deliberately causing some kind of grief to the neighbour, whether mental or physical.

The fourth call in v. 30 insists that it is important not to dispute (*rîb*) with another human, another *'ādām*, without a cause (*ḥinnām*) as in 1.17, especially when no harm has been done to oneself. The verb *gml* has the sense of paying back. Although it is here a separate injunction, it relates very closely to the notion in the preceding verse.

The advice in v. 31 is to not feel envy in respect of one who uses violence for any reason. The second part of the sentence builds on the first by essentially repeating the order—don't copy the violent person's behaviour! Presumably one might be tempted to think that the bully gets what he/she wants, so such behaviour can have its appeal for one whose aim is to exert power over another.

It is to be noticed that no motive is attached to any of these prohibitions—we cannot know what would motivate a person to act in these ways unless it was out of immaturity or to intimidate the other by being assertive. Each of the injunctions is general but most appropriate in the early education of a young person.

3.32-35 As was the case in v. 26 where the preceding negative commands were followed by a *kî*-clause relating to the character or nature of YHWH as understood, so here. These four verses provide a Sage's justification for the preceding injunctions grounded in the Israelite vision of the divine nature; it uses the formal wisdom pattern of the bicolon. In these examples, how the Lord is expected to respond to the ways of the wise and the fool is set out in contrasting lines, until the final verse in which a more general statement about wise and fool rounds out the list. These justifying statements are not 'promises' but reflect traditional views of the nature of Israel's God, here used by the Sages as incentives to urge the young to take the advice seriously. Imperfect verbs are suggestive of an ongoing state. The section derives from the simple Deuteronomic frame of 'blessing' and 'curse' to add force to its explanation—see Deut 7.12-16.

Verse 32 opens with a genitive phrase *tô ͑ᵃbath yhwh* that translates as '(that which is) an abomination to/for the Lord', not 'the Lord's abomination'! It is an objective genitive. It applies to one who is *nālôz*, perverted or devious. In contrast, the 'upright ones' are close and intimate. There is a Confucian saying that approximates this sentiment: 'Great Man is affable and unlike others; Petty Man is like the others, but is also a source of discord.' (君子和而不同; 小人同而不和)。

In v. 33 a contrast is drawn between the wicked and the righteous, with the Lord's 'curse' (*mᵉ'ērāh*) said to fall on the 'house of the wicked', suggesting the wide or collective punishment meted out to the family of the wicked over against the blessings that should flow to the righteous.

It is those who in v. 34 scorn or show contempt (*lēṣîm*) for others who would be scorned by the Lord, while those who are humble are shown divine favour (*ḥēn*), as in v. 22. The opening particle, *'im*, is unusual, normally introducing a conditional clause. Such a view is not entirely impossible here if read as 'If to the scorners he…, then (*wᵉ*) to the humble…' understood to mean 'with/with reference to…'.

It is the final v. 35 that rounds out the lesson to the young. Honour is said to come to the wise as their inheritance or reward, while disgrace is the lot of those who are foolish, not just foolish but stubbornly so, who do not learn. While there appears to be a clear use of Deuteronomic language in these verses, the Sages knew that there was no guarantee that attending to their advice would ensure such a clear and definite outcome. However, they did need to offer some incentive to those receiving instruction, so the verbs are to be read as volitional, expressing what the Sage longed to see happen based on their understanding of the Lord and his nature.

There is some question about the meaning of the participle *mērîm*, from a root that normally refers to something being exalted, hence 'honour'. How it fits here is unclear, though the possibility is that it is a scribal error.

PROVERBS 4

4.1-9 Fifth Address

Listen, children, to a <u>father's</u> instruction, and listen carefully to learn understanding.
Because I provide good instruction, **do not** *abandon my teaching.*
When I was a child to my <u>father</u>, one timid and special to my <u>mother</u>,
He taught me and said to me, Keep your mind fixed on my words, hold fast to my commandments and live.
<u>Acquire wisdom, acquire understanding</u>. **Do not** *forget and* **do not** *turn your back on the words of my mouth,*
Do not *abandon her and she will keep you, love her and she will protect you.*
The beginning of wisdom: <u>acquire wisdom and in all you acquire, acquire understanding</u>!
Elevate her and she will raise you up, she will honour you when you embrace her.
She will place on your head a lovely garland, she will crown you with a glorious crown.

There are a number of challenges for modern readers and interpreters in this Address: (1) Is it the *Voice* giving the advice generally, or is it a father himself speaking directly to his own children?; (2) understanding the shift from domestic instruction in vv. 1-5 to a more general note about Wisdom's gifts in vv. 6-9; (3) noting a high degree of repetition, and dependence on the verb *qnh*, 'acquire', in vv. 5, 7 that is unusual; (4) accepting numerous differences between the Hebrew text and the LXX translation that raise other questions; (5) that specific examples of wise decisions and actions are lacking, leaving the impression that this is more like an Introduction to an Address, rather than an Address *per se*. In short, it would appear that this portion of text has a complex history that is now essentially impossible to unravel, yet individual phrases are meaningful and fully consistent with the instructional aims of the collection overall.

4.1-5 The opening summons to 'Listen', *šim'û* in v. 1 differs from other Addresses in that it is spoken to a gathering of children (*bānîm*), not just to one child. The dominant view in the commentaries is that these are a father's words to his own children. However, it also can be read as what I have called the *Voice* speaking generally of the kind of wisdom training that any parent would be expected to have given his or her children. If it is the *Voice* speaking, then it is the Wisdom tradition itself that then speaks in first person in vv. 2-5.

The verb *šām'a* denotes a broad concept in which hearing is only the initial step, for it also assumes a positive response, a heeding of the advice given, hence also 'obey'. The parallel root *qšb* means paying close attention to matters. Both positive exhortations are followed up by a negative imperative *'al ta'a zōbû*, 'Do not forsake…' in v. 2.

An initial *kî* in v. 2 could be the emphatic 'Indeed…', or 'Because…', giving the reason for the strong call to attend. The speaker argues for the high quality of the instruction given as the reason for not ignoring the teaching. The adjective 'good' (*ṭôb*) carries the sense of advice that is valuable, most practicable, and in accordance with the tradition. Here *torah* does not mean 'Law', but has its broader sense of something to be learned. The verb 'abandon/forsake' (*'zb*) speaks of a deliberate turning away rather than just forgetting or being unmindful of what was taught.

Verses 3-4 open with the same *kî* particle as in v. 2, but with a slightly different nuance, being a reference to time or occasion, so 'When…', referring to the speaker's past when young and under his father's instruction and his mother's special care. The expression *rak weyāḥîd* pictures an only child, not necessarily spoiled, but one who is shy and beloved, especially here by his mother, the phrase *liphnē 'immi* referring to his mother's adoring view of him. That was the time that he was taught that he must ensure that the father's words were held fast in his *lēb* 'heart/mind'. The imperative *šemōr* 'keep/observe' is a verb used frequently with regard to *miṣwôth*, commandments or orders, here meaning the 'father's' orders. To do so could lead to 'life', i.e. the ideal manner of satisfying living.

4.5 contains two positive and two negative commands: v. 5a is in positive mode, but the repetition of the verb *qnh* is unusual as it breaks the pattern of using parallel verbs. Here the verb *qnh*, 'acquire, obtain', suggests putting effort into gaining something, i.e., both 'wisdom' and 'understanding'. The second half-verse turns to negative forms and counsels against forgetting or turning away from 'the words of my mouth'. Oral instruction would have been the main means of teaching by both parents and Sages in a society that was largely non-literate.

4.6-9 The tone of the Address moves from exhorting children to ensure that Wisdom's advice is heeded to appraising the inherent value of

Wisdom itself. The two major terms are *ḥokmāh* and *bînāh*, but the comment moves to third-person verbs and suffixes in contrast to the first-person address as used in 1.20-33. The purpose of the address is to provide incentives for embracing wisdom, for not abandoning her. Wisdom's incentives are expressed in figurative language—it 'protects' and 'guards' one who lives out her precepts.

Verse 7 opens with a phrase *rēšit ḥokmāh* the syntax of which is problematic but contains echoes of 1.7. Whether *rēšit* speaks of priority in time or of importance, of a beginning or starting point, is uncertain, but whichever is the more 'correct' understanding, the command is to acquire (*qnh*) *ḥokmāh* no matter what else one acquires. The heavy use of the root *qnh* repeats that in v. 5 when encouraging the young to 'acquire' wisdom. There does seem to be some textual issue in these verses, but suggested amendments are usually arbitrary and not necessarily convincing. (While non-native readers of an ancient language can usually spot what *to them* are certain problems in a text, it is inadvisable to determine what might have been a correct text without some strong supporting textual evidence, usually from the LXX.)

The encouragement to gain wisdom continues in v. 8 using the imagery of raising something to a higher level, or according it higher value (*sll*), with the assurance that to do so may result in one being exalted or given higher recognition. The verb *t^erôm^emekkā* speaks of causing one to be 'elevated' in some manner whether socially or psychologically. Similarly in v. 8b, wisdom should bring honour to (*t^ekabbēd^ekā*) the one who 'embraces' (*ḥbq*) her, using the figure of close physical contact. The *kî* particle can have conditional or temporal sense here.

The Address closes with yet another incentive from the *Voice* or father, using a different set of images, perhaps drawn from a marriage context, or even that of a physical contest. Garlands and a crown for the head were signs of honour bestowed or won, signifying what should ensue for the one who chooses and acquires Wisdom. Wisdom confers direct benefits to the individual who attends to her advice offering personal satisfaction and community recognition, a reputation as a well-rounded or complete human being who demonstrates the ideal, what Confucian thought calls the ideal person or 'Great Man' (君子).

4.10-19 Sixth Address

Listen, my child, accept my words, and may the years of your life be many.
I have instructed you in the way of wisdom, I have directed you in the straight pathways.

When you walk may your steps not be restricted, if/when you run may you not stumble,
Hold firmly to instruction and do not let go, protect it for it is your life.
Do not walk the path of the wicked, nor walk the way of evildoers.
Keep away from it, do not traverse it, turn from it, and pass it by.
For they cannot sleep unless they have done evil, they are robbed of sleep if they do not cause one to fall.
Truly, they 'eat the bread' of wickedness and drink the wine of violence.
But the path of the righteous is like bright light at dawn, getting brighter until noon.
The way of the evil ones is like darkness, they are not aware of what may cause them to stumble.

This well written and unified Address falls neatly into three parts: vv. 10-12 as an introduction; vv. 13-15 as the central admonitions; vv. 16-19 as supporting evidence or motives for choosing the 'right' path.

The *Voice* again speaks using the metaphors of 'paths', 'ways' and the 'walk', as in 2.8-20, contrasting the way of the righteous, the Dao (道), with that of the wicked, and the safety of the straight/smooth path over that which could cause one to stumble.

The Address is introduced by two imperatives, *šim'û*, 'hear/listen', and *qaḥ*, 'take/accept', followed by the wish that the child may as a result have a long life, longevity being a highly regarded sign of blessing. In v. 11 the speaker reminds the child that he has been instructed in wisdom's 'way' (*derek ḥokmāh*), a way characterized as 'straight' (*yōšer*), though the basic sense is that following the advice epitomizes a life that is 'upright'. Verses 10-11 outline the ideal situation of a child prepared with the guidelines for a long and 'rewarding' life. For Confucius, wisdom offers enjoyment and a full span of life (知者樂，仁者壽).

Verse 12 then expresses the wish for the student child, namely that he/she may walk the way without hindrance, and even if it involves 'running', there hopefully will be no risk of stumbling. While the metaphors of ways and paths are readily understandable, along with the verb relating life to a walk, what might the notion of 'running' (*rûṣ*) mean in this context? It is a rather odd verb to use in the context of living out one's life. It is best viewed as a 'figurative extension' from the notion of walking, to emphasize the point that nothing can cause one to stumble on the 'way' if wisdom, as learned, is applied. Could the verb have been chosen for euphony with the 'ṣ' sounds (*lō'-yēṣar ṣa'ᵃdekā*) that precede it, and possibly making for easier memorization?

4.13-15, the central portion, is powerfully admonitory with four negative imperatives and three positive imperative forms all combining to issue the sternest of warnings never to choose the path and way that are the avenues of the wicked and evildoers.

The sub-section begins by affirming the importance of *mûsār*, 'instruction', and the need to hold to it firmly, never letting go. There is a slight inexplicable grammatical issue here in that the noun is masculine while the related pronouns are feminine, but there is no mistaking the call's intent. The notion of *nṣr* 'guarding/protecting', i.e., to ensure one is taking care of something, like the one watching over the vineyard or the city, is used often with regard to following wisdom's advice—see 2.8; 3.1, 21; 5.2; 7.10. To do so should assure of a full and meaningful 'life', as v. 10.

Two synonymous negative imperatives in v. 14 warn against following the way of the wicked. Two separate but related terms appear in this verse identifying the wicked: *rᵉšā'îm* and *rā'îm*. While there is little doubt about the first term and its sense of immorality and lawlessness, the second term often refers more broadly to disasters or troubles, suggesting that here it could refer to those who cause trouble to others rather than to some more personal moral failure.

Verse 15 refers to the road or way of the wicked as something to be avoided, the root *pr'* meaning to refrain from some activity, while the second verb *śṭh* calls for one to turn away from an object, so here implying a deliberate choice not to follow the way of the evil person. The verb *'ābar* is used twice, with slightly differing senses; the first use is the negative command not to traverse along the path chosen by the wicked, and the second use meaning to pass it by, i.e., choosing an alternative route.

In vv. 16-19 explanatory clauses provide several reasons for not following the path of the wicked. The first reason is spoken of in terms of 'sleep', presumably referring to the evil ones' debased conscience—it suggests that unless they have done something hurtful or caused serious injury to another, they cannot sleep comfortably; only when they have done harm can they relax. What kind of a person is such a one? Certainly not someone schooled in wisdom! Verse 17 changes the figurative language to that of eating and drinking, a person's two basic needs, that in the case of the evildoers is focused on 'eating the bread/food' that is wickedness and 'drinking the wine' that is violence (*ḥamas*); only wickedness and violence sustain these persons. The use of the noun 'bread' here may also carry the nuance of a payment made for advice that is, to say the least, suspect (see Amos 7.12). The imperfect verbs here speak of habitual or ingrained behaviours. The verb *lḥm* that is used in this verse is a rarely used term, not to be confused with the homograph that refers to war and fighting. It is largely confined to several appearances in Proverbs—see 9.5; 23.1, 6, also Deut. 32.24, all poetic uses. The sense appears to approximate an English expression, ‘they will taste…’, connoting the results of a very negative experience.

Verse 18 highlights ‘the way of the righteous’, using the analogy of a light that grows ever brighter. In contrast, the wicked person’s path is compared in v. 19 to deep darkness in which any who choose to walk will encounter unseen causes of stumbling. There are some minor syntax issues in these two verses, especially around the *waw* connector, but not such that the point being made is affected negatively; emendation suggested by some commentators is not required for the sense to be clarified.

4.20-27 Seventh Address

My child, pay attention to my words, incline your ear to my sayings.
Do not lose sight of them, keep them in your mind,
For they are life to those who find them, and healing to all his flesh.
Guard your mind above all else for from it life emerges;
Turn aside from crooked speaking and may sly talk be far from your lips,
May your eyes look to the future, your gaze be straight ahead,
May the path your feet tread be straight and all your ways be secure.
Do not veer to the right or to the left, turn your feet away from evil.

There are elements in this Seventh Address making it clear that it is a discrete unit, one in which the *Voice* emphasizes that it is Wisdom’s words that are life-giving and healing. The Address consists almost entirely of imperative statements in both positive and negative cast, and it lacks a concluding statement such as appears in other Addresses—see 2.21-22 and 4.18-19 that resolve with a generalized contrast between the wise and the fool. One conspicuous rhetorical element used is the reference to body components—ears, heart/mind, mouth, flesh, lips, eyes, and feet—in metaphors for the child/student’s complete ‘embodiment’ of the ‘wisdom way’. Strangely, perhaps, the term *ḥokmāh* itself is not present. Many of the central verbs and other literary components used throughout conform with those found in other Addresses, including the formal introduction in v. 20 (cf., 5.1).

After the opening address, the verb *qšb* calls for close attention to be paid, as in 4.1; 5.1; 7.24; it is one of the many verbs calling for attentiveness, but whether it is more specialized than the verb *šm‘*, ‘listen/obey’, is unclear. Here it balances the use of the phrase ‘incline the ear’ (*haṭ-’oznekā*), an idiom for listening carefully.

Verse 21 begins with the negative order not to lose sight of wisdom’s words and sayings, balanced with the positive order to ensure that they are kept in one’s heart. The expression *b^e^tôk l^e^bābekā* calls for the words to be stored in the depths of one's heart or mind. There is no obvious reason why the noun should take this longer form rather than the simpler *lēb*—see v. 23. The call is followed by the assurance in v. 22 that they are the source of 'life' to all those who 'find (*māṣāʾ*) them', an unusual expression in the context of being taught them. The second half of the bicolon turns inexplicably to third-person singular, 'his flesh'—or is it a generalized one's flesh?—and the assurance that the words of the Sage can bring physical healing, or at least 'good health'.

Imperatives resume in v. 23 with a call that essentially repeats that in vv. 21-22, though using more forceful language, noting the heart as the keeper of that which gives life. The initial phrase, *mikkol-mišmār*, is literally 'from every prison…', clearly a figurative expression that here seems to refer to the act of guarding rather than the place that is guarded. The initial preposition *min* carries the sense of 'more than…'. The point is clear that the heart (here *lēb*), one's mind, must be guarded above all—see NRSV 'with all vigilance'—because it is the storehouse and source of life or life-giving advice. For *ḥayyîm* 'life' see notes on 2.19. The noun *tôṣ*ᵉ*'ôth* from the root *yṣ'*, 'go out/leave', hence 'source'—I have rendered it as life 'emerges'—is feminine plural, but its subject is masculine, a slight grammatical inconsistency.

The following verse turns to speech and the metaphors of the mouth (*peh*) and lips (*s*ᵉ*pāthayim*) to call for crooked and devious speech, for lies and dishonest speaking, all to be abandoned. It does not necessarily imply that the child is currently using such speech, but more generally, that such speech should not even be entertained.

In v. 25 it is the eyes that are used as examples. In the second half verse the parallel noun used is the rare term *'ap'appayim*, eyelids. The verbs here speak in terms of looking straight ahead (*nōkaḥ*), looking forward, i.e., as directional, but the sense is figurative, most likely referring to looking out for potential causes of stumbling, to be aware of one's need for an upright (*yāšār*) manner of living. The two verses that follow, vv. 26-27, build on this call for keeping to the Wisdom path and not diverging in any way, to right or left. One's walk needs to be stable and one's feet must be kept from walking on any but the right path. The verb *nāṭāh* in v. 27a is similar to the verb *sûr* in v. 24 and v. 27b, both of which speak of figuratively 'turning aside' and thus taking an alternative course of action, usually implying a failure to keep Torah in its broadest sense.

Proverbs 5

5.1-23 Eighth Address

This Address contains a number of difficulties arising from what appears to be a somewhat disjointed collection of miscellaneous sayings and advice about sexual relations. Despite this, it can be divided generally into four sub-sections: 5.1-2 serve as an introduction to the Address, similar to each of the preceding addresses; 5.3-14 relate to the theme of avoiding any contact with a certain kind of woman, one who is not a member of one's own household; 5.15-20 focus on being faithful to one's wife, or to the women of the household; 5.21-23, by way of conclusion, speak more generally to the potential fate of the wicked.

5.1-2

My child, pay attention to my wisdom, listen closely to my understanding,
To preserve prudence, and may your lips guard knowledge.

The opening words in 5.1 are almost identical to those in 4.20; there the objects of the verbs were spoken matters, here they are more specifically defined as wisdom and understanding. These latter terms, 'my wisdom' and 'my understanding', are abbreviations for '*the wisdom I have taught (you)*' and '*the understanding I have provided*'. They are summary terms for all that the *Voice* has passed on to the student. See also 2.1-2.

The syntax of 5.2 is unusual in that it begins with an infinitive construct 'to keep/preserve' (*lišmōr*). Its function is to explain what paying attention and listening closely will enable, namely, that the student/child might always act with prudence. It is followed by the hope that the 'lips', or what the student speaks about, will assuredly be truth, not folly or anything false.

5.3-14

For the lips of an 'outsider' woman drip with honey, her speech is smoother than oil,

But in the end, she is as bitter as wormwood, sharp as a two-edged sword.
Her feet lead down to death, and her steps proceed to Sheol.
(She does not follow a path of life, her pathway wanders and she/you do not know (it)?).
But now, children, listen to me and do not turn aside from (heeding) the words of my mouth.
Stay far from her way and do not approach the door of her house,
Lest you give your strength to others, your years to the merciless,
Lest strangers consume your strength, and your labour goes to the house of the stranger.
At your end you would bellow as your flesh and body are consumed.
And you would say, 'Oh, how I hated discipline and my heart despised reproof!'
I failed to listen to my teacher's voice or listen closely to the ones instructing me.
For a time I was in all kinds of trouble in the presence of the assembled congregation.'

From the 'lips' of the student to the 'lips' of the temptress, the *Voice* warns the student to be aware of the dangers to 'life' inherent in her enticing words. The woman in question is generic, here described as a *zārāh* individual—see notes on 2.6-10. Clearly she is not one from within the household with whom sexual relations were possible, nor is she designated a prostitute, a class of woman that was not necessarily regarded as evil or as outside society's bounds. There clearly are negative overtones in this *zārāh* description, but the obvious implication is that the woman is a temptress, so the adjective is a slang derogatory term. Her 'lips' are described as 'dripping honey', sweet talk, smoother than (olive) oil. The noun *ḥēk*, 'palate', is a metaphor for speech, parallel to 'lips'.

Two similes are used in 5.4 to describe her, contrasting the sweetness and smoothness of her oily words as in reality both bitter and sharp. The similes are traditional, using a bitter herb, wormwood (*la'ᵃnāh*), to characterize her speech, and sharpness like that of a two-edged (double mouthed) sword that can slice in both directions. The use of *'aḥᵃrît* has both temporal and locative sense, emphasizing that one's latter end or fate, as in v. 11, is dismal, leading to death, not life. That fate is outlined more explicitly in 5.5-6 with the claim that her feet, or her way, leads only to 'death', to Sheol, the place of the dead. The plural noun *ḥayyîm* refers to a manner of living—see notes on 2.19. Verse 6 presents several difficulties that have troubled commentators over the generations and no satisfactory solution is available. The *pen-tᵉpallēs* phrase, normally would mean 'lest she/you(sg) take heed…' and *lō' tēda'* 'she/you(sg) do not know…' are obviously problematic given the subjects are uncertain, but any emendation suggested is arbitrary and unsupported by other compelling evidence. It is advisable to bracket the translation offered and move on, since the note of warning is already quite clear in the text more generally.

There is some question about v. 7 in its present location given that it appears to intrude between vv. 6 and 8 that clearly refer to the 'woman', while v. 7 appears to introduce another address, one directed to more than one student. Unfortunately there is no evidence to support any potential emendation so readers can only work with what appears to be an anomaly. While grammatically there is some inconsistency, and the feminine object in v. 8 requires clarification, it does fit the general context. See the same plural form in 7.24.

5.7-8 introduces three imperatives following the initial call to pay attention, the first in v. 7b and the third in v. 8b, both in the negative, i.e., they are matters to be avoided. The first requires the children not to turn aside from the words they have been taught, and the third warns them not to approach even the entrance of the *zārāh* woman's house. The intervening call in v. 8a is to ensure that their 'ways' are far from that of the woman.

Verses 9 and 10 follow the preceding three imperatives with reasons for listening to the advice offered, namely, two warnings introduced by the particle *pen*, 'lest/otherwise…' The first potential loss is giving one's 'glory' (*hôd*) to 'others (masc)', a cryptic expression capable of various interpretations: loss of dignity, strength, self-respect. The parallel phrase *šᵉnōthekā lᵉ'akzārāy*, '(giving) your years to the merciless' is equally cryptic, leading again to a variety of potential situations. It is not possible to identify more specifically what the 'strangers' (*zārîm*) and 'the house of the alien' (*bēth nokrî*) refer to if they do not refer to elements within the *zārāh* woman's household. The 'lest…' clause of v. 10 speaks of strangers (male) in the house of the alien taking their fill (*śb'*) of one's strength and labours (*'eṣeb*) i.e., capitalizing on someone else's life and work. The *nokrî* term may refer again derogatively to the woman. In the context of v. 14 where it is clear that the person regrets or groans (*nāham*) as a consequence of such loss and now faces embarrassment before the congregation, it would seem that the point being made is that one's reputation would be so sullied as to be irrecoverable. The *'aḥᵃrît*, 'at your end…', or perhaps 'in the end…', refers to a subsequent reaction, not necessarily the end of one's life. It relates to one's flesh and 'meat' (*šᵉ'ēr*) coming to an end, figurative for wasting away, a manner of living that is 'deadly'. The Hebrew text in these two verses is obviously somewhat cryptic, so translation and interpretation are tentative.

Verses 12-14 reflect a chastened student expressing regret at not having taken to heart all that had been taught about such a woman and the trap she constituted, for it has impacted on his current standing within the community. The two terms, *qāhāl* and *'ēdāh*, are apparently synonymous and refer to the *gathered Israelite community*, assembled for one of many purposes, be it for war or worship. Here the phrase appears to be more general—being looked down upon by the community, no matter how small, would be socially unbearable.

5.15-20

Drink water from your own well, flowing water from your own source,
Your springs might gush forth in streams in public places.
Let them be for yours only and not for the outsider who is with you.
May your fountain be blessed, and bring joy from the wife of your youth.
A lovely deer, a graceful doe, may her breasts satisfy you always, in love of her may you be constantly enthralled.
Why should you be enthralled by the non-family woman, my son? (Why) cleave to the bosom of the stranger?

This section should not be read from the culturally inappropriate perspective of western monogamous marriage!

Rather than general advice to one's student, these verses are specifically aimed at the family man, the head of a household, calling for his fidelity to the women in his household. Metaphors and figurative language give a highly poetic cast to the issue of sexual behaviour that was considered culturally acceptable.

Verse 15 is a sophisticated verse, beginning with a popular saying that is then applied in a figurative way to the realm of sexual pleasure. To 'draw water from one's own well' is part of a known description of living the idyll—eating grapes from one's own vine, figs from one's own fig tree, and drinking from one's own water supply (Isa. 36.16). That idyll represents domestic peace and pleasure. However, here that saying is used figuratively, the 'flowing (water)', *nōzᵉlîm*, and 'one's own source' (*bᵉ'ēr*) referring to sexual activity—see also Song 4.15.

In v. 16 we note some issues that, while clearly relating to the matter at hand, raise problems of interpretation. NRSV regards the verse as a question, implying a missing interrogative at the beginning of the verse, and the imperfect verb *pwṣ*, 'scatter', seems purely descriptive of the man's actions with regard to his ‘springs’ (*m‘yn*). That ‘they’, his semen, could be scattered in the streets or outside areas—the sense is that ‘outside’ (*ḥûṣāh*) refers not to a location but to a forbidden relationship—is a warning or threat rather than a promise or simple statement. This reader considers the imperfects here to speak of potential results, namely that illicit relations could result in children being born outside the family circle. In view of the fact that in many Israelite households there were several ‘wives’ and/or other females with whom the master could have sexual relations, one must consider that the advice or warning issued here relates only to relations with a woman who is not within the man’s family unit—with one who is *zārāh*, an outsider, as her child would be. See notes at 2.16.

The advice in v. 17 is in one sense confusing. The initial call is clear—keep your ‘spring’ to yourself, i.e., keep it within the family. The second half of the colon raises questions in that the negative counterpart, *zārîm*, is masculine, perhaps implying men in the woman’s family who would claim any child born.

The *Voice* then invokes a blessing on the man’s ‘fountain’ and urges that he derive (physical) pleasure from his wife with whom he has been for many years, described as *’ēšeth n^{e}‘ûrekā*—see 2.17.

Verse 19 takes up the metaphors of the ‘doe’ (*’ayeleth*) and ‘deer’ (*ya$^{‘a}$lath*), two animals that in love poems represent certain commendable feminine qualities—see Eccl. 2.7; 3.5. Presumably they are generalized references to a man’s wife, said to be ‘loving’ and ‘gracious’. The advice then turns to the physical with the call to find solace, to pleasure in her breasts, to be totally overcome, satiated with her love constantly.

The section then closes in 5.20 with a rhetorical question—Why would you, my son, be infatuated by the *zārāh* woman, embrace the bosom of the ‘outsider’? The *Voice* presents this action as both unthinkable, when one is sated with a wife’s love, and unimaginable, when considering the dangers such an outside liaison represents. No more foolish an act is conceivable!

5.21-23

Indeed, a man’s ways are ever before the Lord’s gaze, and all his paths he surveys.
May the evil deeds of the wicked trap him, and entangle him in the cords of his sin.
May he die for his lack of discipline, besotted in his many sins.

The thoughts or beliefs expressed in these three verses are of a very general nature. They appear unrelated to the specific topic of the preceding verses, especially as they turn to a religious dimension with a unique reference to Yahweh and a belief in his constant regard for human affairs. The tone is almost threatening. The noun *'îš*, 'man', represents the individual, not necessarily only males. Yahweh is presented as constantly aware of (*m^{e}pallēś*) how an individual's 'way' accords with the tenets of Wisdom. The implication is that this divine awareness then allows the Lord to respond to one's conduct appropriately, and reward or punish. These verses concern the deeds of the evil (= foolish) individual and so it represents a stern warning that metaphorical 'death' is folly's only reward.

The initial *kî* I read as the asseverative, 'Indeed/Truly', rather than 'For' as providing a reason or explanation for the foregoing. Given that these verses are very general, there is no absolute reason to connect them so directly to the foregoing discussion of sexual (mis)behaviour.

Using the figure of entrapment with ropes or cords in v. 22, two religious terms, *^{a}wônôth*, 'evil deeds', and *ḥaṭṭā'h*, 'sin', speak of general foolish behaviour for which Yahweh is constantly on watch. There is in this belief that humans are under constant surveillance a measure of thought-control or fear-mongering, trying to frighten the young into a mode of living; there is a subliminal cast as the Sage is reminding the child that YHWH is forever keeping watch. The use of participles in v. 21 and imperfects in v. 22 brings it all into the ever present.

The final two verses I read as volitional, rather than as promissory statements, the imperfects *yilk^{e}dunô*, 'trap' and *yāmûth*, 'die', figurative for whatever punishment, i.e., disastrous outcome, ought to follow one's many follies (*'iwweleth*). It is this volitional dimension that gives the *Voice* a degree of authority in its attempt to convince the young to accept and live by its advice. As Confucius noted also, '…whoever offends (sins against) Heaven has no court of appeal' (子曰 … 獲罪于天，無所禱也).

PROVERBS 6

6.1-19 Wisdom's Warnings

This section of the book consists of four easily identified, discrete sub-sections that have little connection with the material in the preceding chapters; each is formally and content-wise independent, but with the introductory 'My child, …' in 6.1 marking it as a new collection. Whether the sections existed as some smaller collection previously or were independently gathered and placed here by the final editor of the Book is impossible to determine, so speculation is unfruitful.

The four sub-sections are: 6.1-5 related to the folly of making pledges; 6.6-11 deal with the danger of lapsing into poverty if one is lazy; 6.12-15 point to a calamitous outcome for one who is deceptive, whose word cannot be relied upon; and 6.16-19 that uses the numerical form (x, x+1) to itemize and denounce a range of detestable behaviours.

6.1-5 Unwise Pledges

> *My child, if you have made a pledge to your neighbour, (and if) you have committed yourself to an outsider,*
> *You are trapped by the words of your lips, captured by the words of your mouth.*
> *This is what you must then do, my child, to save yourself for you have fallen into your neighbour's power. Go and plead with your neighbour.*
> *Don't let your eyes fall asleep nor your eyelids close*
> *Save yourself just as the gazelle escapes from the hand (of a hunter), and as a bird from the hand of the fowler!*

The *Voice* addresses the young/student, setting out a potential situation. It basically deals with the range of relationships one might have with a neighbour, with the verb *'ārab* relating to doing business, making promises, offering to act as guarantor and generally committing oneself to being of help. The *Voice* issues a warning—If (*'im*) one were to stand guarantee for another, then one is entering a potentially 'dangerous' situation—one is bound by one's word/promise.

The first issue is to determine whether the neighbour (*rēʻa*) and the outsider (*zār*) in v. 1 refer to one and the same non-family relationship (see my note on *zār* in 2.16). This reader is choosing to read the two nouns as parallel terms for the one person, a non-family neighbour. While some have questioned the *l*ᵉ preposition's direction—is it a pledge 'to' or 'for/on behalf of'?—the simplest view is to read it as between the 'child' and the neighbour direct.

The syntax of v. 1 is ambiguous. While it is likely that v. 1b is also under the influence of the opening conditional, and thus a second version of the condition (see NRSV), that is not necessarily so; it is also possible that v. 1b is the first element in the statement of the apodosis, hence the brackets in my translation above.

While making the pledge may be a friendly and neighbourly thing to do, the *Voice* urges caution in v. 2: be aware that you have made a commitment that you must keep, for you are now under obligation—'captured' (*lākad* as in 5.22) is the language used here—to one who is outside the family. On the other hand, while the wiser move would have been never to make such a pledge, IF (*'im*) you have made one, go quickly, don't sleep on it (v. 4), go and find a way to release yourself before it is too late. The second verb in v. 3 (*rps*) is unclear but the context suggests it is a call to speedy action, though some see it as more a call to humble oneself. Verse 5 then uses two examples to emphasize the need to escape 'the hand' = power (of the hunter?). The examples are 'like the gazelle (*kiṣbi*)', or 'like the bird' that escapes the hand of the bird-catcher.

The advice in this bare and seemingly universal statement appears to preference anti-social and selfish thinking, an attitude antithetical to Wisdom's more communal concerns. To read it as a general warning would mean that Wisdom was entirely opposed to acts of kindness or assistance, surely not a correct perspective. The absence of wider context gives the advice a rather negative cast when it most likely intends only to warn against making *rash* promises or foolish commitments—see 12.18; 20.25, similar to the advice of Qoheleth in another context (Eccl. 5.1-7). Any commitments or oaths sworn should be made thoughtfully and carefully, fully aware of their implications.

Committing oneself to a course of action unthinkingly is regularly advised against in Wisdom literature, and Confucius too was aware of this as a potential problem: 'In serving a prince, rashness brings disgrace; among friends, estrangement' (事君數，斯辱矣，朋友數，斯疏矣).

6.6-11 Contra laziness

Go to the ant, lazybones; watch its ways and wise up!
Lacking any leader, officer, or ruler,
It stores up (food) during the summer, gathers its food during harvest.
How long would you lie there, you lazy one? When would you awake from deep sleep?
A little (longer) sleep, a little (longer) slumber, a little folding of the hands in bed,
And poverty will arrive like (one trampling), and loss like a man with a shield.

Already in this book we have seen nature used as exemplars of behaviour from which humans can and should learn (1.17; 5.19). So the reference to *ants* as examples of wise conduct is unsurprising.

Laziness is one of the personal traits that offends the Sage—see Prov. 10.26; 24.30-34; 30.25; Eccl. 10.18—for it inevitably has negative consequences leading to poverty and loss, something that diligence and hard work can forestall. Failing to learn that lesson, even to learn from a small insect like the ant, is sheer folly.

The section is a stand-alone piece in this setting, its content unrelated to the surrounding material.

Using imperatives, the *Voice* challenges the lazy person (*ʿāṣēl*) to 'go' and to 'observe' the ant and its 'ways', this latter being code for a manner of living (see 2.12-20). Observing and reflecting are the basic tools of trade for one who would become wise.

Verses 6-7 outline the characteristics of the ant's 'way', namely, an apparently leaderless ant fully engaged as part of a collective, preparing a store of food for the coming winter. The behaviour demonstrates forethought, co-operation, and diligence to achieve the goal of his and others' very survival.

In contrast to the ant stands the lazy person who is challenged again to get up and follow the ant's example. The use of *ʿad-māthay*, 'how long…?' in v. 9, normally expressing distress at prolonged suffering in the Lament psalms (see Pss. 4.2; 13.1), catches the *Voice's* longing for the lazy individual to get up and stop being a fool, lying about and achieving nothing. The balancing second half of the verse provides emphasis.

In v. 10 the text has room for two possible readings: (a) they are the words of the *Voice*, mocking words, as three times the *Voice* stresses sarcastically how 'little' (*m^{e}ʿaṭ*) sleep, slumber and 'folding of the hands' can lead to poverty and loss (v. 11); (b) they are the words of the lazy person who is responding to the 'how long?' question with the request to stay in bed just that little longer. The first possibility is a statement of fact in line with Wisdom's values. If option (b) is intended, then it is necessary to understand an initial implied request, '*Let me...stay* a little longer...'. Commentators are divided as to which reading to prefer. The phrase 'folding of the hands' signals readiness to sleep; it appears in Ecc 4.5 in the context of a fool's laziness, a refusal to act.

The *Voice* finally, in v. 11, warns the lazy person of the inevitable consequences of his laziness, namely inescapable poverty and loss. Those consequences are expressed in terms of two analogies: one is that poverty comes like a 'vagabond(?)' (*m^{e}hallēk*), a vagrant, someone who wanders about, a homeless person, but perhaps meaning that such is the result of poverty; the other is that it comes like 'a man (of/with) a shield' (*'îš māgēn*), perhaps implying as a warrior bent on attack. The latter term is of uncertain meaning, but together the two similes convey a sense of inevitability and threat. So, to the lazy soul, 'Wise up!'

For Confucius, laziness was also an issue of concern: 'A gentleman who prefers his own ease/comfort is no gentleman' (子曰：士而懷居，不足以爲士矣).

6.12-15 The Deceiver

A scoundrel, an evil man goes about with perverted speech,
Winking with his eyes, shuffling his feet, pointing with his fingers.
Deception is in his heart, plotting evil the whole time, constantly sowing discord.
Therefore let calamity befall him without warning, suddenly be broken beyond healing.

There are several issues of detail within this passage of text with some terms of uncertain meaning, and physical actions in v. 13 of unclear purpose or function, while the overall sense of deliberate deceit nevertheless remains clear.

A series of participles dominates vv. 12-14 in a description of a wicked person that comes to a climax at the end of v. 14 with a charge that the one described is intent on 'sowing discord', causing conflicts in the community. The list opens in v. 12 with the phrase *'ādām b^{e}liyya'al* in which the person is labelled as evil, one of the 'sons of Belial' (2 Sam. 22.5-6), a mythical demon connected with death. Adding to the description is the phrase *'îš 'āwen*, 'a man of evil', a double indictment, for he is one who goes about with 'crookedness of mouth', an idiom for speaking in a manner that intends to deceive. The use of the adjective 'crooked' (枉者) to describe the non-upright person is frequent in Confucius.

In v. 13 there are three physical references—eyes, feet, fingers—and participial forms describe each. The eye is said to be 'pinched', the root *qrṣ* applicable to pinching dough, hence presumed to refer to winking. The real issue is knowing what that sign could possibly mean in that ancient culture; the context allows one to assume it is not positive. The feet are said to be *mōlēl*, but the root appears to be a homograph offering three quite different meanings—speak, scrape, wither (BDB)—with 'scrape' the more likely sense here. However, again, what that action possibly connotes is not obvious to a modern reader. The third participle *mōreh* involves the finger, so some kind of 'pointing' seems a logical interpretation, though the root *yrh* itself is usually related to 'teaching'. Once again, the cultural significance of the action is uncertain, but has to be assumed to be negative since they are descriptive of the scoundrel (*'ādām b^{e}lîya'al*) and villain (*'îsh 'āwen*).

Verse 14 appears to consist of three phrases: deception in the heart; plotting evil; sowing discord/causing quarrels. The closing verb is an emphatic piel form of the root 'send' (*y^{e}šallēaḥ*). Added to these charges is the temporal phrase *b^{e}kol-'ēth* that dramatizes all as constant activity.

The section closes with the *Voice* expressing a desire to see calamity come upon such a person as just described. I read the verb *yābô'* as volitional. Such calamity is unexpected but imminent and to result in a situation that cannot be reversed, cannot be 'healed' because it will 'shatter' (*yiššābēr*) the one who is evil.

6.16-19 What the Lord Hates

There are six things the Lord hates, seven that to him are an abomination.
Haughty eyes, a lying tongue, hands that shed innocent blood.
A mind/heart that plots evil plans, feet that hasten towards doing evil.
One who lies by testifying falsely, and one who sows discord between brothers.

This section makes use of a sequential numerical form (x, x+1), one of several such forms to be found in Proverbs and elsewhere (see Prov. 30.7-31; Amos 1.3–2.8), here using the consecutive numerals 'six' and 'seven'. The common theme of the items is stated as matters that offend the Lord, then the seven offending actions are listed. As in the preceding section, physical body parts are used figuratively—eyes, hands, heart, feet—representing the whole person. The shared physical focus of the section, together with its closing reference to 'sowing discord', probably account for its placement alongside vv. 12-15. Both sections are obviously independent and have their own history, but are now editorially placed alongside one another.

The use of numerical wisdom forms is well-known throughout the ancient N.E. Wisdom writings as well as in other collections, such as Chinese wisdom (see *Postscript*), suggesting that there might well be a common element in the reflective processes that order the minds of any who are engaged in the challenge of understanding and educating citizens for a better personal and community experience. The purpose of the consecutive (x, x+1) double form rather than the single numeral form is generally unclear other than heightening the x+1 numeral itself that identifies the concerns of the moment.

The eyes (v. 17) are described as *rāmôth*, in which the root *rwm* 'high, rise up', also implies pride and arrogance, haughtiness, looking askance at others. The tongue, a figure for one's speech, tells lies, while the hands shed innocent blood, they are means of violence against the innocent. Together these human instruments when used to threaten, to demean, to do violence are utterly offensive to Yahweh. In v. 18 two additional physical instruments are named—the heart, the core of the mind in Israelite thought, and the feet representing the path being trodden—are both identified as components in the wicked person's plotting or planning to exert evil influence on others.

The final two detestable qualities (v. 19) are listed as 'giving false testimony' and 'sowing discord', the latter also central in v. 14. All seven 'sins' are social offences that can bring harm to both the individual and the community, but in the context of a theocentric community such as Israel was, the offences are understood to be more serious as they are offences against its God.

6.20-35 Ninth Address

My child, keep your father's commandments, and do not abandon your mother's teaching.
Bind them on your heart permanently, tie them around your neck.
Whenever you are out walking let it (the heart) be your guide, when you lie down may it watch over you, and when you awake may it speak with(in) you.
For the commandment is a lamp and the teaching a light, and the way to life is (in) the reproofs of discipline
To preserve you from the evil(?) woman, from the smooth tongue of the 'outsider' woman.
Do not let your heart long for her beauty; do not let her capture you with her eye(lashes),

> *For a prostitute's fee is as little as a loaf of bread, but the wife of (another) man may demand a man's very life.*
> *Can fire be carried in one's bosom without it burning one's clothes?*
> *If one walks on hot coals will his feet not be scorched?*
> *Just so will the one who goes to the wife of his neighbour. Anyone who touches her will not go unpunished.*
> *They do not despise a thief when he steals to satisfy his hunger*
> *But when caught he pays seven times, he must hand over everything in his house.*
> *One who commits adultery has no sense, the one who does so destroys himself.*
> *He will meet harm and disgrace and his shame will not be wiped clean,*
> *For jealousy arouses a husband's anger, and he will show no mercy when he seeks revenge.*
> *He will not accept compensation and will refuse any bribe no matter how great.*

The Address this time returns readers to the matter of the 'outsider' woman (see 5.3) whose wiles should be resisted, and to the parental instruction to be heeded (as also in 1.8). The unit presents via a range of special literary features that may suggest a complex back-story. There is a degree of disjunction between the literary units involved, but all cohere around the general topic of the dangers of being drawn into any relationship with the 'outsider' woman. How the Address came to its present form is no longer clear, and 'solutions' offered to some of the textual challenges within do not add greatly to a better understanding of the passage as a whole.

As to the structure of the Address: vv. 20-22 can be read as an Introduction; vv. 23-24 justify the value of the teachings provided and of their purpose; v. 25 warns against the wiles of the female; vv. 27-28 present two rhetorical questions using 'burning' as a theme to affirm an outcome that is applied in v. 29; vv. 30-31 seem at first glance to be unrelated, but do raise the issue of punishment or consequences, before returning to the matter of adultery and its potential devastating and inevitable impact on all parties (vv. 32-35).

Verse 20 is almost a duplicate of the call in 1.8 as the *Voice* commends the parental guidance and its importance. That importance is stressed in vv. 21-22 by way of a summary of daily activities to underscore the need for their teachings to be ever in mind, no matter what the activity (see also 3.3). It has long been recognized that vv. 21-22 echo similar expressions noted in Deut. 6.6-8; 11.18-19. Both versions locate the heart, i.e., the mind, at the centre of the call to 'bind' (*qšr*) the teachings or the Law to the physical person; both use the '*walk,..., lie down,..., awake,...*' formula to cover the activities of daily life. The rhetorical similarity points to the language used as formulaic, widely-used in different literary contexts.

The father's commandments and the mother's *torah*, if kept, can have the effect of leading, protecting and advising. The on-going value of parental instruction in v. 22 is presented in three temporal clauses, but there is a change from plural nouns in vv. 20-21 to singular in v. 22, the change perhaps to be explained as referring to the 'heart' singular. I read the three imperfect forms in v. 22 as volitional rather than as 'promises', so '*may/let it…*' in order to stress the potential benefit of heeding the advice now locked away in one's heart.

The explanation follows in the three verbless phrases of v. 23a with both the commandment and *torah* described as providing 'light'—both *nēr*, 'lamp', and *'ôr*, 'light', are well-used figures that speak of insight and understanding. To these is added the 'reproofs of discipline' (*tôkᵉḥôth mûśār*), signs of divine love according to 3.11, that define the way of life, or the life-giving way.

It is in v. 24 that the specific function of the commandments and *torah* are identified—the leading, protecting and instructing that come from the heart are 'to preserve you…' (*lišmorkā*), to keep you away from what the MT refers to as *'ēšeth rā'*, 'evil woman'. The adjective *rā'* is perhaps an error for *rē'āh*, 'neighbour', as in v. 29, supported by the use of *nokriyyāh* in the second half of the verse that NRSV unfortunately renders as 'adulteress' when she is better described as the 'outsider' woman—see notes on 2.16. It is her 'smooth tongue' (*ḥelkath lāšôn*), her smooth talking, that embodies her temptation.

Two warnings are issued in v. 25—the initial one warns against allowing *one's own* desires to determine action, the second more defensive, preventing *her* wiles from capturing one's desires. The woman's beauty and her use of it—her 'eyelashes' designed to allure—must be resisted.

It is the reference in v. 26 to a 'prostitute's fee' that seems out of context since there has been no allusion to the woman as a *zônāh* previously. The conclusion to be drawn is that this is a general note about the comparatively cheap demand of the prostitute over against the enormous cost of a dalliance with a neighbour's wife. The mention of 'bread' (*leḥem*), a slang expression for a small payment for services rendered—see also the same term applied to lying prophets' payments (Amos 7.12)—contrasts with the loss of one's 'life' if/when entangled romantically with the wife of another. Although this general understanding of the verse's intent is agreed, some details are uncertain. The use of *bᵉ'ad*, 'for', perhaps 'in the case of…', raises the issue of the prostitute's minimal demand—a loaf of bread. On the other hand, the *'ēšeth 'îš*, 'woman of a man', or a married man's wife, can exact a *nepheš y^eqārāh*, something more precious, the man's very life/being.

Two rhetorical questions follow in vv. 27-28. They both appear to be traditional question forms that highlight the inevitable danger of foolish action: carrying fire in one's bosom will burn one's clothes, and walking barefoot on hot coals will surely burn one's feet. In the present context their function as examples of dangerous behaviour is obvious, and so they strengthen the warning against foolishly being taken in by one's own desires or by the woman's sly temptations. The questions serve to introduce the point being made that a man who sleeps with—literally 'touches'—the neighbour's wife (*'ēšeth rē'ēhû*) will inevitably have to pay the price. The phrase *lô'yinnāqeh* in v. 29 signals that he won't escape the consequences whatever they are, or by whomever administered.

Verses 30-31 present a challenge in the sense that suddenly the topic turns to the punishment of a thief as exemplar for the punishment that should befall the adulterous act—vv. 32-35. The general statement that a thief who steals to assuage his hunger is not despised, presumably is because his was regarded as an act of self-preservation. On the other hand, if he is actually caught stealing, then he will be punished severely, even to the extent that he loses his home. There seems to be some missing information here or some disconnect, for verses 30-31 hardly fit together logically. One possible approach might be to read the imperfect *yignôb* as frequentative, meaning that he was often known to steal—is his impoverished state well known in the community? However, v. 31, if he is caught in the very act of stealing then he must pay, and pay seven times the worth of what was stolen. That fine is quite ridiculous if the man was genuinely hungry for he is said to have a house and possessions that could be appropriated to cover his crime. There clearly are some issues with the details in these verses, but the principle of having to pay when caught in a foolish relationship with the wife of a neighbour remains a valid point. The issue of payment does not depend on legal argument but arises simply from a man's foolish action, a folly that is destructive.

In v. 34 there is mention of the offended husband's jealousy; he is sure to seek unrestrained revenge, though it is unclear whether that would apply to the offending man as well as towards his wife. Most regard it as applying to the man who according to Law should be put to death (Lev. 22.10). Payment of a 'gift' (*šōḥad*) may be a bribe to avoid the death penalty. However, there is some question about the details in this final sub-section other than the warning that fooling with another's wife will inevitably end badly for the offending man, and perhaps also for the wife involved.

In the Confucian Analects there is rarely any mention of sexual matters though the term used, 色, has a semantic range that is very broad, so interpretation and connotations are very much context dependent. However, there is one saying that addresses sensuality or lust more generally; in things to be avoided it lists '…sexual intercourse while still too young and before the pulse—literally 'blood pressure'—has settled down…'(少之時，血氣未定，戒之在色).

Proverbs 7

7.1-27 Tenth Address

This reader views this Address as consisting of three parts: vv. 1-5 as the Introduction to the Address; vv. 6-23 as an inserted imaginary narrative about a young man being seduced by a woman, and the potential cost of his dalliance; and vv. 24-27, a further call or warning that such activity leads to 'death' as its conclusion. It is a well-constructed piece, with the inserted narrative almost certainly a once-independent foreign-sourced tale representative of those used by sages and teachers when instructing young members of the community. As an insertion, one can expect that there will be some minor disjunction between its details and the application made of it. See below.

7.1-5 Avoid the 'Outsider' Woman

My child, keep my words and secrete my commands within you,
Keep my commandments and live, and my torah as the apple of your eye.
Bind them on your fingers, write them on the tablet of your heart,
Say to Wisdom, 'You are my sister'. Call insight your relative.
To protect you from the 'outsider' woman, from the stranger with her smooth speech.

The formal literary elements of an Introduction to the Address appear again here, virtually identical to those in 2.1; 3.3; 4.1, 4; and 6.20, indicating that the Editor(s) was very familiar with the language that was associated with the form. Verses 1-4 are marked by eight imperative forms, with v. 5 explaining the calls as offering a way to protect one from the 'outsider' woman and her smooth speech. The dominant verb in the Introduction is *šāmar*, 'keep/protect', used with both nuances.

In v. 2 the phrase '*the apple of your eye*', i.e., the pupil of the eye, represents something prized for its value (see Ps. 17.8), in this case, Wisdom's *torah*. Binding the commands and instruction to one's fingers as one would wear a ring is one figurative aide-memoire, similar to 3.3, along with the suggestion that the commands be figuratively engraved on the heart as on tablets of clay or stone, i.e., a permanent record.

The imperative in v. 4 to name Wisdom as one's 'sister' is paralleled by naming 'insight' as a close relative (*mōdā'*), the two metaphors together representing how close one should keep the wise instruction received. While the language of the calls is unusual—especially when considering the use of 'sister' as lover (Song 4.9-11)—there is no reason to read them as extraneous, as somehow inconsistent with the rest of the text. The Introduction then concludes in v. 5 with the explanation that keeping wisdom's instruction as close as a 'sister' would protect (*šmr*) the young from an 'outsider' woman with her smooth but deceptive talk. In 2.16 the same purpose is noted using the verb *nṣl*, 'rescue'. See notes on 2.16 relating to the description of the woman and her 'outsider' identity.

7.6-23 The Temptress

'For from the window of my house, through the latticework I looked out
and saw among the simple, and noticed among the young one who lacked sense,
(he was) passing along the street near her corner on the way to her house.
In the twilight, in the evening as the dark of night (descended).
Then a woman approached him, dressed like a prostitute, and with clear intent(heart)
She was loud and wayward, never staying at home.
At one time in the street, at another time in the square, at every corner she waits.
She seized him and kissed him and brazenly says to him:
"I had to make an offering, and today have paid my vows,
So now I have come out to meet you, looking forward to seeking you, and I have found you.
I have covered my couch with coverings, coloured spreads of Egyptian linen,
I have sprayed my bed with myrrh, aloes and cinnamon
So come drink our fill of love till morning, let us delight in making love.
For my husband is not at home, he is off on a far journey.
He took his bag of money with him and will not return until full moon."
She swayed him with her seductive speech, with smooth talk she leads him on
Straightway he follows her and goes like an ox to the slaughter, or (like a stag(?) to the trap).
Until the arrow pierces his liver. He is like a bird flying into a snare, unaware that it will cost him his life.'

In this central portion of the Address the *Voice* inserts an imaginary, but perhaps typical, scenario of a naïve young man being seduced by a scheming and practiced married woman. (In the LXX version it is the woman, not the *Voice*, who looks out from her own window and spies the young man.) It begins in first person, implying that the *Voice* is speaking from personal observation and emphasizing the very real possibility of such a scenario. It then describes an imaginary conversation between the woman and young man. The final two verses, vv. 22-23, stress the danger to 'life' that such behaviour brings.

The woman (v. 10) in this inserted and imaginary tale is not the woman mentioned in v. 5, but is representative of the challenge that the *Voice* seeks to address, namely the folly of forbidden sexual activity.

The initial *kî* in v. 6, usually rendered as 'For…', does not have any explanatory function but is a marker indicating the change of direction in the account—it is an editorial link, perhaps best regarded as 'Indeed,…' It pictures one looking out on one youth among a group of young people described as 'simple ones' (*pᵉtā'yim*) in a typical village scene. The reader is to imagine that the young ones are playing about in a carefree manner with one of them acting foolishly (*ḥᵃsar-lēb*), literally, 'lacking in mind'—see also 6.32. He is pictured walking along the road 'near her corner', meaning that he is in the vicinity of 'her' house (i.e., of the woman to be introduced in v. 10). He walks 'the way to(wards) her house'. There is nothing sinister in this situation, no apparent intention on his part to meet with her. Verse 9 places the scene late in the day, as it gets dark. There is some question about the term *'îšôn*, 'time'(?), that is very rare, but the general sense is that it is growing dark, so the scene is set in the gloom at the end of the day.

'Lo and behold' (*hinnēh*) a woman approaches the lad. She is dressed as a 'prostitute' (*zônāh*), apparently in something distinctive and representative. That she is 'wily' is assumed—the phrase *nᵉṣurath-lēb* contrasts with the state of the youth's heart (v. 7)—and her character is outlined in vv. 11-12 where she is described as a loud and wayward extrovert. These two renderings are not certain as *hōmiyyāh* and *sōrar* depend largely on cognate languages for their possible meaning, suggesting that the inserted narrative (vv. 6-23) was of foreign origin. However, it is clear that they envisage a woman who seems well-known for her nightly activities, sometimes in the street, sometimes in the town square or the corner, because 'her feet' are never at home—her sandals are often under someone else's bed. She is, according to the narrative, something of a predator—no doubt this is all editorial imagination creating the scenario.

In v. 13 she makes her intentions clear by seizing the youth and brazenly, or 'with hard face' (*hē'ēṣāh pānehā*), kissing him. Then her 'smooth words' begin as the *Voice* creates a narrative of her seducing the youth, vv. 14-20.

The woman makes a statement about her religious obligations just having been fulfilled, so she now has set her mind to meeting the youth—not just any youth, but this one in particular—how smooth! The sacrifices mentioned, *šᵉlāmîm*, usually indicate peace offerings, thank-offerings, but here their specific purpose is unclear. Verse 15 begins with *'al kēn*, 'Thus/therefore', suggesting that she feels released from her religious obligations and so can now 'get back to work' as it were with her primary interest, seeking and finding impressionable young men to seduce. The *Voice* imagines her invitation to the boy—an invitation for him to come to her home as she has prepared a beautiful and sensual environment for love-making. The couch has been perfumed with myrrh, aloes and cinnamon and the best of Egyptian linen laid out for a night of love-making. The lad need not worry about the husband coming home unexpectedly, as he is on a trip to some far location, having taken enough money for the venture. Some commentators suggest it was a business trip, buying the spices or linen (?), but that assumes too much and there is no need to be precise—this is, after all, the *Voice's* imagination speaking. The husband won't be back for some time—'until full moon' could mean 'up to a month' later, assuring the youth they will not be interrupted, and the dalliance discovered. The noun *kēse'* for 'full moon' is rare, only elsewhere in Ps. 81.4. With this the speech ends and the application follows in vv. 21-23.

So, the young man, captivated by the invitation, on the spur of the moment (*pit'ōm*) follows the woman home, 'like an ox to the slaughter'; he is an innocent, unaware of the consequences of his actions. A second simile compares him to an eager stag(?) running blindly towards a trap, however, because the original Hebrew is essentially unintelligible any meaning depends on textual emendations; the suggested reading simply seeks a comparable simile to the one in the previous line—hence the brackets in my translation above. The animal does not expect that it will be speared with an arrow. The third simile is of a bird flying into a snare or net across its flight path; it likewise is not aware of the danger ahead. In this final example the narrative returns to the threat to life that such forbidden sex can invoke; the lad is ignorant of the danger, captivated by the adulterous wife. It is presumed that the 'loss of life' motif is figurative, but see also 6.34-35.

7.24-27 The Way to Sheol

And now, children, listen to me, and attend to the words of my mouth.
Do not allow your mind to turn aside to her ways, do not wander into her paths,
For those she has laid low are many, her victims numerous,
Her house is the road to Sheol, leading down to tombs of the dead (death).

The Address concludes with a further call to the children (pl.) to listen and take note of what they have heard. It is introduced by the 'And now…' phrase, *wᵉ'attāh*, as in 5.7, while the following call uses the verb *šm'* in place of *šmr* that dominated the opening call. It also uses two negative imperatives in v. 25 similar to those in 5.7-8—verse 24b reverses the imperative of 5.7—before setting out the main reason for issuing the warnings (vv. 26-27). The vocabulary of the section echoes that found in 2.18-19 and 5.5-6.

The first negative imperative in v. 25 calls for the young not to allow his heart/mind to 'turn aside' (*'al-yisṭ*) to 'her ways'. The 'her' is not specified, and so in this context may refer back to the adulterous wife in the imaginative narrative (vv. 6-23), or to the initial 'her', the woman in v. 5; it is a general call to be careful when approached by any woman outside the family circle, not to 'stray' and be taken in by 'her'.

Given that this is a concluding and general call, it is important to understand v. 26 as applying to all 'outsider' women. Some commentators have suggested that it is the woman of v. 5 who is now accused of having murdered countless men—a suggestion resulting from mistakenly identifying the generic 'her' so specifically. Rather, as a general warning it alleges that there have been so many men who have fallen into the trap set by the kind of woman here identified. The use of the verb *hrg*, 'kill', is not to be read literally but is figurative of the 'death' described in v. 27. Other commentators have read this text from the mythological point of view, of 'death' (*māweth*) as representing the god Mot, suggesting that it warns against Canaanite religious activity. However, the point being made surely is analogical, that 'her house' (and its forbidden sexual activities) was to the living who entered what Sheol and its chambers were to those already dead (as also 2.18; 5.5).

Proverbs 8

8.1-36 Wisdom Speaks Again

A brief preface in 8.1-3 introduces Wisdom in the third person in tones reminiscent of 1.20-21, but the chapter is then dominated by Wisdom's personal testimony in first person speech in vv. 4-31. The latter can be divided into vv. 4-11, 12-21, 22-31. In vv. 4-11 Wisdom calls to the community, addressing in particular the foolish. She claims that her words are 'straight' and 'righteous', that she is more valuable to an individual than silver and gold; in vv. 12-21 she speaks of aspects of her own character, her insights, her qualities, such as her role as counsellor to royalty (vv. 15-16); in vv. 22-31 she makes the extraordinary claim that she was the first of God's creative acts and thus was the agent through whom the Universe was established! The claim is far more broad than that in 3.19-20. Essentially, Wisdom is here 'selling' herself and her incomparable attributes to any who would listen. Her presentation is much more developed and much more encompassing than that in the opening chapter. The *Voice* speaks in vv. 32-36 to close the chapter, contrasting with the adulteress in ch. 7.

8.1-3 She Calls

Is it not Wisdom that calls, and (is it not) understanding that speaks up?
On the top of the heights, along the way, at the crossroads she stands,
By the gates at the entrance to town, at the entry points she shouts.

The *Voice* introduces Wisdom via a rhetorical question that asserts the ubiquity of Wisdom—she is everywhere, and throughout the community announces her mission, the verbs emphasizing the power with which she announces both her presence and her message.

While the similarity with 1.20-21 is clear, here in 8.1-3 there is evidence of a different literary background as it uses some unusual idiomatic terms in v. 3—*yad-šᵉ ʿārîm*, literally 'the hand of the gates', and *pî-qeret*, 'the mouth of the town', with *qeret*, a possible Canaanite term very rarely used in the Hebrew Scriptures, in lieu of the more usual *'îr*, 'city'. What specific religious background these verses might have is uncertain—many assume a Canaanite context, the significance of which is vague, other than some kind of linguistic connection—and any speculation arbitrary. However, the figures of 'hand' and 'mouth' are readily understandable—the 'hand' is a figure of that which is alongside (2 Sam. 18.4), the 'mouth' that of an opening (Josh. 10.15).

The rhetorical question as a positive statement with which the chapter opens is statistically unusual—there is only one other use of the form in chapters 1–9—see 6.27. Wisdom and Understanding both make their presence and message known in all quarters of the land—on the heights, in the streets, at the intersections, by the gates, and at the entrance to the towns, entrances or doorways, there Wisdom 'shouts' (*rnn*) its message. Nowhere is beyond the call of Lady Wisdom.

8.4-11 Wisdom's Value

Understand, you simple ones, (what is) prudence, and you fools set your mind aright,
Listen, for I am speaking of noble matters, and from my lips comes uprightness,
Indeed, my mouth speaks the Truth; and evil is an abomination to my lips.
All my words are just, none is perverse or crooked.
They are all straight to one who has understanding, and upright to those who have acquired knowledge.
Accept my discipline in lieu of silver, knowledge in place of choice gold.
For Wisdom is better than jewels, whatever you long for cannot compare with her.

The personified Wisdom, using first person speech, addresses the community, as in 1.20-33. We have already noted that Wisdom's personification is a feature unique to the biblical context and unknown in Confucius—see 'Lady Wisdom' in the Introduction. The notion that Wisdom herself speaks out is actually a rhetorical device, for it is the Sages themselves, the real personifications of Wisdom, who were charged with teaching and advising, calling the community to listen and learn. Two unusual terms are used in v. 4—*'îšîm*, a rarely used plural form that speaks of all 'men', or everybody, along with the phrase *b^{e}nē 'ādām*, 'sons/children of Adam/mankind'. This is a universal and unrestricted call that in v. 5 addressed only those who are regarded as simple, meaning the young, the immature and naïve, together with the 'foolish' (*k^{e}sîlîm*), those who wantonly disregard Wisdom's advice.

The phrase *hābînû lēb* in v. 5 is problematic. The verbal element is identifiable as calling for understanding, but the link with *lēb*, 'heart/ mind', is difficult to comprehend. The LXX text would suggest a possible different but very similar original written form—*hkn* in place of *hbn*—giving a more understandable call to 'set your heart aright', or similar. It is possible that the MT is here slightly corrupt, though the LXX text varies enough from the Hebrew generally that it cannot be relied upon to be maintaining the 'original' version of any statement.

In v. 6 the noun *n*^{e}*gîdîm* 'nobles/princes', or 'noble matters', seems an unusual term to parallel *mēšārîm*, things that are upright or straight, but there are no grounds to emend the text as some have suggested. The point surely is that what Wisdom teaches is something of great and positive value that needs to be heard and acted upon. The call to 'Listen up' is then justified in vv. 7-9 for Wisdom's advice is not only of value, it represents truth (*'*^{e}*met*), a claim supported by a series of descriptors—her words are just/righteous (*ṣedeq*), not crooked or perverse, they are straight (*n*^{e}*kōḥîm*) and upright (*y*^{e}*šārîm*). Each of these points to Wisdom's claim to the highest ethical standards, because she vows that evil (= foolish) words will never pass her lips. Another unusual expression is in v. 9b, the reference to ones who 'find knowledge' (*mōṣ*^{e} *'ê da'at*), perhaps meaning those who have 'discovered' and thus experienced the true value of her advice. When Confucius speaks, he says: 'All three hundred poems may be summed up in one phrase, "Let your thoughts be righteous [no evil]" (詩三百， 一言以蔽之，曰： 思無邪)'.

Verses 10-11 address Wisdom's claim to be of real and incomparable value, a value that exceeds that of jewels, of silver and gold, or of any material normally considered desirable (see also 2.4; 3.14-15). So, she makes an offer to all, inviting them to 'accept' (*q*^{e}*ḥû*) or 'take' her discipline and knowledge in lieu of all else. The full expression should read *q*^{e}*ḥû-mûsārî w*^{e} *'al q*^{e}*ḥû kāsep* but the repeated imperative is implied.

8.12-21 By me kings rule

'I, Wisdom, have dwelled with Prudence, and I have attained knowledge and foresight.
To fear the Lord is the hatred of evil, pride and arrogance (is) the way to evil, deceptive speech I hate.
To me (belong) counsel and insight, I have understanding, I have power.
By me kings rule, and potentates dispense justice.
By me princes rule, and nobles, all who judge justly.
I love those who love me, and those who seek after me will find me.
Riches and glory are mine, enduring wealth and righteousness.

My fruit exceeds gold, fine gold, and my produce better than choice silver.
I walk in the way of righteousness, along the paths of justice,
I endow those who love me with wealth and I would fill their treasuries.'

Wisdom's address continues, here citing in particular her personal positive qualities, with a heavy emphasis on first person pronouns. It is a speech marked by many verbless or nominal statements. She speaks of herself not only as the source of wisdom and prudence, but also as the source of power and wealth, of justice and righteousness. The 'pride and arrogance' she eschews as the road to evil (v. 13) seems to be overlooked in her self-adulation!

In v. 12 commentators have been troubled by the phrase 'dwelled (in/with) prudence', suggesting minor textual adjustments to give what is then thought to make sense. This reader is generally reluctant to emend the Hebrew text 'to make it fit', unless there is some more concrete evidence available, and here that is lacking. 'Prudence' is an abstract equivalent to wisdom, so to claim that they 'live' together or co-habit, seems perfectly sensible. The use of a perfect verb form, *šākantî*, describes the reality of their intimate relationship. In that relationship Wisdom has 'found' knowledge and foresight, reading the imperfect *'emṣā'* as an on-going state of being.

The phrase *yirath yhwh*, 'fear of the Lord', in v. 13 is identical to that in 1.7, where it is the starting point for gaining wisdom; the phrase here can be understood as a subjective genitive correlating with a hatred of evil (*ra'*). What breeds evil is a person's pride and arrogance. The verse itself, built around the verb 'hate', is regarded by many as an addition of general interest, or a scribal insert that breaks into the list of very personal attributes with its more general statements about Wisdom in vv. 12, 14-17. The fact that the verse consists of three colons rather than the regular two is seen as the primary evidence for it being originally extraneous, but there are several other examples of three-colon verses in these chapters, not all of which require being treated as inserts—see 1.27; 4.4, 5; 5.19; 6.22; 7.22, 23.

Verse 14 returns to the listing of personal attributes claimed by Wisdom; they are reminiscent of the four similar attributes that are ascribed to God in Job 12.13—advice (*'ēṣāh*), wisdom (*tûšiyyāh*), insight (*bînāh*), and strength (*g^ebûrāh*). What is the collection saying by comparing Wisdom's attributes with those of God? See also Isa. 11.2 where they are royal attributes. Clearly these four attributes together form a standardized body of terms relating to authority figures, representatives on earth of the divine, in an idealized community. In them Wisdom celebrates its practical and existential value alongside the numinous; the invisible God thus becomes real in Wisdom's advice.

Political power dominates the claims of Wisdom as counsellor in vv. 15-16. Whether kings, princes, rulers, judges, or any other leader, all derive their authority and power from Wisdom, she says, and they exercise it in the pursuit of justice (*ṣedeq*) and righteousness (*ṣ^edāqāh*).

An emphatic announcement about love appears in v. 17 (*'ănî... 'ēhāb*), raising a slight textual issue as to whether the object is 'those who love me', or 'those who love her'. The context would suggest the former, the Q're form, as more contextually appropriate. See also v. 21. 'Love' as meaning 'appreciation' differs markedly from 'love' as used elsewhere in these chapters where it relates more to sexual relations.

The provision of material riches (*'ōšer*) and honour (*kābôd*) emanate from Wisdom (v. 18) as do enduring wealth (*hôn 'ātēq*) and 'prosperity' (here as *ṣ^edāqāh*, but see also v. 20). While that may be the broad claim, there is no guarantee that they always and unremittingly flow to those who seek her and live out her instruction.

In v. 19 the outworking or result of following Wisdom's advice is depicted figuratively as its 'fruit', its 'produce', and claimed to be of greater positive value to one's life than any material substance such as gold or silver, as in vv. 10-11. The Confucian sayings are identical, emphasizing magnanimity, sincerity, diligence and graciousness (恭, 寛, 信, 敏, 惠) as the superior gifts that Wisdom provides.

The moral quality of *ṣ^edāqāh* 'righteousness', is uppermost in v. 20-21 where the sense is of a pathway or manner of lifestyle devoted to justice (*mišpāṭ*). It is a lifestyle that promises to provide material wealth (*yēš*) to those who 'love me'—see v. 17. The noun *yēš*, 'wealth', occurs only here in the Hebrew Scriptures. The imperfect forms of the verbs in these two verses appear to be firm promises. However, sage advice could not assure any such outcome, so I choose to render them as volitional = 'I would provide...', reading the imperfect *'ămallē'* as a volitional, not as a definite promise.

8.22-31 Wisdom and Creation

The Lord created me (at) the outset of his work(way), the first of his deeds of old.
From ages past I was established, from the first, at the origin of the earth,
When there was as yet no deep waters I was brought forth, as yet no springs of abundant water, Before the mountains had been set up, before the hills were shaped, I was born,

> *When he had not yet made the land and the outdoors, the first dust of the soil,*
> *When he set up the heavens I was there, when he drew a circle on the face of the deep,*
> *When he made firm the heavens above, when he established the fountains of the deep*
> *When he assigned to the sea its limits, and the waters should not go beyond his command, and marked out earth's foundations,*
> *I was(?) beside him (like a master worker), I was(?) day by day his delight, rejoicing before him constantly,*
> *Rejoicing in his earthy world and delighting in the children of Adam.*

This independent unit is remarkably different from the preceding. In vv. 12-21 Wisdom is 'selling' herself by claiming a wide range of superb personal qualities and powers, and in particular providing potential material wealth and riches. Here in vv. 22-31 it is Yahweh who dominates and Wisdom plays a secondary role, that of an agent created by Yahweh. Lady Wisdom is, according to the clear meaning of the text, a quite independent entity who, having been 'created', then participated with the Lord in the establishment of the material world, though some read the text as meaning simply that Yahweh in his wisdom created the world. Perhaps the distinction is subtle, but it is one to be noted. The text is clearly an independent version of Israel's creation tradition with echoes of Genesis 1–2, Job 38, and Psalms 93 and 104. While there are numerous creation traditions in surrounding cultures that speak of gods bringing the world into being, the version recorded in 8.22-23 is clearly one of Israel's own.

Among the rhetorical elements that feature are the many temporal phrases, especially a series of time-related adverbs in vv. 22-23—'before', 'from ages past', 'from the beginning', 'at first', 'at the outset'—while in vv. 24-29 there are six examples of the preposition *b^e* with an infinitive construct indicating temporal clauses, 'When he (YHWH)...'. There is also a chiasm in vv. 30-31 involving 'rejoicing' and 'delighting' that round out the poem—see details below.

Verse 22 opens with YHWH as the subject, to mark a very distinct turn away from Wisdom herself. The verb *qānānî* is key. However, its application requires unpacking. While many translate the verb as 'create', there is very little evidence (e.g. Ps. 139.13) that points in that direction from its more basic sense of 'acquire/possess', as happens in Gen. 4.1. If context is primary in deciding meaning, then 'create' is here a legitimate option, suggesting that a root *qnh* may well be a homograph with two separate semantic values.

The phrase rendered '(at) the beginning of his work' (*rē'šît darkô*) uses the noun *drk*, normally 'way/road', but again context suggests 'his work/task' is intended (see also Job 26.14). The noun *rē'šît* is 'the first/chief', so 'the outset', emphasizes Wisdom's priority. Although the syntax is abbreviated, the second half of the verse makes the full sense obvious, namely, that it is prior also in terms of time—'before his deeds back then' (*qedem mip'ālāyw mē'āz*) the Lord was at work.

Similarly, v. 23 continues the theme of priority with three phrases—*mē'ôlām*, *mērō'š*, and *miqqedem*—all prefaced by the preposition *min* to leave no doubt as to Wisdom's temporal priority. The verb in this verse, *nissaktî*, is of disputed origin and thus of meaning—the form suggests a Niphal from *skk*, 'weave', but perhaps is best regarded as *nsk*, 'be set up/establish'. An unusual plural form is used in *miqqadᵉmē-'ereṣ*, 'the beginnings of the earth', but one should not read too much into that form.

Verses 24-25 consist of four simple temporal phrases—the first three each beginning with the preposition *bᵉ*, 'in/with/by'—followed by a noun, then a verb. In v. 24 the nouns refer to things that were not yet in existence at the time Wisdom was created—the 'oceans' (*tᵉhōmôt*), and the 'springs of waters' (*ma'yānôt nikbaddēy mayim*). Echoes of Genesis 1 and 7 are present. In v. 25 the presentation refers to things *before which* Wisdom was set up—it predated the mountains and hills. The verb *ḥôlaltî*, 'I was born', is used of Wisdom's existence prior to the creation of both the ocean (v. 24) and the hills (v. 25), clearly with figurative meaning. In the case of the mountains, the verb used is a passive form *hoṭbā'û*, 'caused to settle'. All images in these verses reflect the cosmology of the period.

Verse 26 continues the pre-creation theme but prefers new vocabulary—*'ad-lō'*, 'while not yet...', indicating once more Wisdom's temporal priority. In this example, the land and the 'outside' are parallel terms for land within and outside the city rather than land as opposed to sea. It is balanced in v. 26b by an unusual phrase, *rō'š 'oprôth tēbēl*, literally 'head of dusts of earth/world'. The JPS rendering is 'the world's first clumps of clay', understanding 'head' as figurative for 'first', and *tēbēl* as the earthen world. It is highly poetic.

In vv. 27-29 there are six temporal phrases each introduced by the *bᵉ* preposition attached to a verbal infinitive that carries the third person suffix referring to Yahweh's creative action. The first of these relates to the heavens being 'set in place' (*hᵃkînô*)—see also 3.19. When that action took place, Wisdom says 'I was there'—i.e., 'there' as part of the action, not as a defined location. The second half of the verse refers to an action 'on the face of the deep'. It is described as a dome shaped item (*ḥūg*) being carved or drawn there. Given the ancient cosmology, this suggests setting the horizon line. In v. 28 it is the sky or clouds above (*š^{e}ḥaq*) that are made firm, and the 'fountains of the deep' that are established. Those 'fountains' were pictured as the 'waters below the earth' welling up to produce the great flood in Gen. 7.11. Boundaries were established so that the sea could not overtake the land in v. 29, the waters unable to go against the divine 'mouth/word', and the earth's foundations marked out. That the earth rests on foundations suggests that the cosmology's imagery draws on the notion of it being a building.

There are several issues with v. 30, an unusual tripartite form. The verse features two uses of *wā'ehyeh* in v. 30a and b, following the series of infinitives in vv. 27-29, suggesting that the change has some significance. This reader considers the prefixed imperfects to have frequentative value to emphasize Wisdom's constant presence—*yôm yôm* and *b^{e}kol-ʿēth*—during the creative activity. The initial v. 30a also has a unique noun *'āmôn* found nowhere else in the Hebrew Bible, so its meaning is disputed and subject to a wide variety of interpretations and guesses, some quite fanciful, especially the 'child' option. There is a Hebrew noun *'ommān* 'architect', hence 'master builder' (Song 7.1), supporting NRSV's rendering as such, but that makes Wisdom too much of an actor. Otherwise, one might consider a derivation from the root *ymn*, 'to be at the right hand', consistent with the claim to have been 'there'. JPS suggests 'as a confidant' (from root *'mn*). However, if there is some formal relationship between all three elements in this verse, as is customary in poetic lines, then it is highly likely that what is now *'āmôn* would have been some word or phrase with a temporal sense similar to that used in the two parallel phrases. Could it once have been written *yômām*, 'daily'? All suggestions are nonetheless arbitrary given there is no supporting textual evidence. What has to be made clear is that there is no suggestion here that Wisdom was active in the creative task—in this text she was simply 'there' while God was at work.

In Confucius, 天 (Heaven), plays a more benign part, (天何言哉，四時行焉，百物生焉，天何言哉) saying nothing while the four seasons roll on and all living things appear.

There is a chiasm in the final two lines—*ša^{a}šuʿîm—m^{e}saḥeqet—m^{e}saḥeqet—ša^{a}šuʿay*—to emphasize the joy and rejoicing Wisdom felt as a participant in creation. What Wisdom's report omits is any reference to other components of the creation story as told in Genesis, such as plants and animals, together with the sun, moon and stars; it is a much-abbreviated account, though it does conclude with a reference to the creation of humans, the *b^{e}nē 'ādām*, who also post-date Wisdom.

8.32-36 Finding Life

And now, children, listen to me. 'Happy are those who keep my ways.
Listen to instruction and become wise, do not neglect it.
Happy is the one who listens to me, attending each day at my gates, waiting outside my doors.
Indeed, the one who finds me finds life, and obtains favour from the Lord.
But the one who fails to find me (misses) me self-destructs; all who hate me prefer death'.

Here it is not absolutely clear whether it is the *Voice* or Lady Wisdom who is speaking—but see 5.7 and 7.24 for similar calls and language, suggesting that it is probably the *Voice*.

The introduction to this chapter involved the *Voice* noting, in 3rd person, the value of Wisdom and her call made throughout the heights, the way or paths, the portals and entrances of town. That same note of ubiquitous possibility of hearing and learning to be wise re-appears in this conclusion. So the *Voice* again calls on the children/students of the community to hearken to Wisdom's words, assuring them that happiness depends upon both listening, then keeping, her ways and instructions. To do so will help them 'find' life and divine favour, while also warning that there is a destructive path, one leading to 'death'.

Commentators generally feel that this conclusion has a complex history and so offer suggestions as to what rearrangement of lines is suitable as well as identifying what added material there might be. The LXX text does differ from the MT, so there is some substance to this suggestion of a disrupted text. However, 'tinkering' with an ancient text without quite clear evidence in support makes for arbitrary modifications.

The theme of 'happiness' (*'ašrē*) can be said to dominate this conclusion for the one who protects/keeps (*šāmar*) and obeys (*šāma'*) the ways (*derek*) of Wisdom. While the imperatives in vv. 32-33 call for the young persons to attend to 'me', to become wise and not to neglect her, the remainder of the conclusion is more statement-like, relating to general principles and the consequences or outcomes of obeying them.

The use of *'ādām* in v. 34 to represent humanity at large follows its use in v. 31. This is another tripartite line where watching at the doors and waiting at the gate are figurative for seeking opportunities to listen to what the *Voice* has to teach. The doors and gates/entrances are not specified as of the Temple or town, so are figures for the locations where Sages taught.

Verse 35 states the reason for the instruction. The initial *kî* is here read as 'Indeed,...' for emphasis—'the one who finds me, finds life'. The verb *māṣā'* carries the sense of discovering something of great value, defined as 'life' (*ḥayyîm*) to be contrasted with 'death' (*môt*) in the next line. Additionally, favour or an accepting attitude from the Lord is wished upon one, not 'promised'. Here that mark is wisdom's ways, the manner of living that is being taught.

The compact final v. 36 begins with the verb *ḥt'* that is usually translated 'sin' in most contexts. However, the root actually refers to failing to reach a standard, or to miss the mark. Rendering it here as '...miss me' is ambiguous and easily misunderstood—I have suggested '*fail to find me*'. The rendering of *ḥōmēś* as 'injure oneself' is far too tame for the setting—*ḥmś*, violence, is better known today by 'Ḥamas', the terrorist organisation. So, we are looking here at a self-destructive lifestyle, one that threatens one's very being, the *nepheš*.

The contrasting verbs 'hate' (*śānā'*) and love' (*'āhab*) are used deliberately to stress the point being made that those who reject Wisdom's advice are set upon a course that, in the mind of the Sages, will lead to figurative 'death', as in 7.27.

Proverbs 9

9.1-18 Wisdom and Folly

The structure of this chapter can be readily discerned despite questions remaining about its overall integrity. The most obvious element is the contrast between Lady Wisdom in vv. 1-6 and the woman depicted in vv. 13-18, both sections employing shared vocabulary and phrases. Despite the shared language, the contrast is between two personifications—one that gives 'life' (v. 6), and one that leads to Sheol and 'death' (v. 18). Interrupting these two 'case studies' is a collection of more general statements in vv. 7-12 that highlight divergent responses to Wisdom's admonition regarding the wise and the fool. Why these two studies in vv. 1-6 and vv. 13-18 were separated editorially is unknown, and the intruding section hinders rather than helps any search for an answer.

The Hebrew text of the chapter existed in differing versions, some lacking vv. 9-10, and another missing vv. 10-12—see *BHS* footnotes—while the LXX contains additional material after v. 12. It is clear that behind the present MT there is a back-story that is complex and no longer recoverable. However, its location at the close of these initial nine chapters can be regarded as a fitting and representative conclusion.

9.1-6 Wisdom's House

> *Wisdom has built her house, she has cut her seven pillars.*
> *She has butchered her animals, and mixed her wine, she has also set her table.*
> *She has sent out her female servants, and she (herself) calls from on the heights of town.*
> *'You who are simple, come on in here!' She says to the mindless one:*
> *'Come, eat my food and share the wine I have mixed.*
> *Abandon your simple ways and live, walk in the way of understanding.'*

The rather startling beginning of this chapter presents Lady Wisdom as herself having built her house, cut pillars, killed animals, mixed wine, set her table and sent out invitations to a feast, all of which is very dramatic, and all highly imaginary. The verb 'build' is purely figurative as it is most unlikely that 'she' would have built it herself. There are two earlier references to a 'house' in which the noun is a metaphor for a group of wicked persons (3.33) and in 5.8 the imaginary home of the foolish adulteress. There is no preceding text that links Wisdom and the metaphor of a house. While some have speculated that the house represents the Temple—a normal house would not have seven pillars—and others have suggested a cosmological background, all the imagery in vv. 1-6 is pure poetic invention, a grand 'domestic' setting for the imaginary feast that is the real focus of the pericope, the 'house' being merely an appropriate venue. It is ultimately v. 6 that defines what the imagery serves—an invitation to those who are simple or naïve to partake of the food and wine, i.e., wisdom itself, offering 'life' to those who accept. In the second study, vv. 13-18, a woman is sitting at the door of her 'house' (v. 14). The imagery of a 'house' in both case-studies confirms that it is poetic invention. Speculating on a possible source of inspiration for the concept does not advance the poetry.

In v. 1 Wisdom is identified as plural *ḥokmôt*, rather than the singular form—see also 1.20—while the continuing text uses singular forms throughout. Wisdom being a generalized and abstract notion, the reference to it 'building a house' is merely the setting for the 'feast' that she has prepared. More challenging is the second half of the verse in which 'seven pillars' are said to have been cut, the purpose of which is not indicated, thus leading to speculation that is not helpful given the deliberate vagueness of the text. The verb *ḥāṣᵉbāh*, 'hew' or cut, implies large wooden pillars, objects hard to source in Israel—the wood used to build Solomon's Temple had to be sourced from Lebanon. The numeral 'seven' bears some significance as a sacred number, but here in relation to the 'house', the point is unclear, even if one assumes that the pillars were components of the house. If the house has been built—the verb *bānāh* is perfect—the pillars (*'ammûd* from the root 'to stand') may have intended some decorative function rather than underpinning it as some have suggested. However, it is clear that the 'house' is a creative poetic image, the deeper meaning of which, if there is one, is elusive.

The phrase *ṭābᵉḥāh ṭibḥāh* in v. 2 is literally 'she slaughtered a slaughter', understood to mean that she (?) has butchered her animals that then provide the meat for guests at the feast; the slaughter's purpose is not that of an offering or sacrifice. Along with this she has prepared wine to which she has added herbs and/or spices for the feast's two main elements, and has set the table in readiness. All that was then required was to send out the invitations by the hand of her servant girls (v. 3)—these persons also are part of the poetic imagery, not to be mistakenly read as actual people or as identifiable relatives of Lady Wisdom. The second half of v. 3 uses unusual terms—*'al-gappē*, meaning 'from on top of…', and *mᵉrōmē qeret*, 'the heights of the town'. They are used also in v. 14 where, as a component of the rhetorical style used in both case studies, they also describe Folly's call.

An initial *mi-pethi*', 'whoever is simple/naïve' in v. 4 invites people to turn aside (*yāsur*), though the destination 'here' (*hēnah*) is exceedingly vague, so it represents not a specified place but is a call to a change of direction in life. If the invitation to a feast is being offered by servant girls, the scenario as described is not logically consistent, since the verb 'call' (*tiqrā'*) is feminine singular, suggesting that it is Wisdom herself who is speaking. The parallel second half of v. 4 addresses individuals who are *ḥᵃsar-lēb*, literally 'lacking in heart', or who act mindlessly, without thought.

Verse 4 is repeated in v. 16 as part of the rhetorical pattern adopted for the two scenarios, drawing attention to the contrast being made between them.

Wisdom's invitation for the feast is outlined in v. 5. It uses the root *lḥm*, usually 'food/bread', in a verbal mode with the noun form as complement. It is a rare rhetorical feature and mostly confined to Proverbs.

The invitation continues in v. 6 calling for maturity and for living according to wisdom's advice, and in that manner defining what the invitation really means. The food and drink imagery, as all other imagery in the speech, is figurative for living in accordance with Wisdom's advice. It is probably going too far to contrast the feast in vv. 2-5 with the more basic food on offer in v. 17.

9.7-12 General Maxims

Whoever corrects a scoffer wins contempt; whoever rebukes the wicked is hurt.
Do not rebuke one who scoffs lest he hate you; rebuke a wise man and he will love you.
Give (instruction) to the wise and they will become more wise; teach the righteous and they will gain in understanding.
The beginning of wisdom is fear of the Lord and knowledge of the holy ones is insight.
For with me may your days be increased, and may they add years (to) your life.
If you are wise, you are wise for yourself; if you scoff you bear it alone.

Here we have six individual maxims or general statements that represent Wisdom's insights into human life. They speak of the positive advantages of being wise and the disadvantages of being foolish. As noted above, these maxims intrude between the two contrasting 'case studies', that of Lady Wisdom and of Ms Folly. Since each case is essentially the formal reverse of the other, the editorial reason for separating them with this collection of general sayings remains a mystery.

Verse 7 is directed against one who scoffs, who openly devalues or spurns wise advice. The verb used here, *lyṣ*, occurs often in this book, noting its presence in contexts opposing the positive values advanced by Wisdom. The teaching here reminds that one who seeks to correct a person with such a negative attitude to Wisdom will suffer contempt; it is set in parallel with the wicked causing grief to any who would rebuke them, or rebuke their foolish behaviour. The rendering of *mûmô* as 'hurt' or similar is one dependent on the context since the noun has a basic meaning related to that which has a blemish.

The call in v. 8 is similar to that in v. 7 in that it also targets one who scoffs, stating that any attempt to rebuke or correct one such person will result in being hated by them. In contrast, if it is a wise person who is rebuked, that one will appreciate correction and 'love' you for it. The 'love/hate' contrast is typical of Wisdom's advice that prefers to use simplistic language for maximum effect—see also 8.36.

Another truism is found in v. 9 as both wise and righteous individuals are said to benefit from advice or correction, and each will grow as a consequence of being corrected. The imperative 'give' (*tēn*) lacks an object for some reason, but the context suggests it would be something within the realm of wisdom instruction or 'advice'.

Confucian thoughts on this matter are much alike in that correcting another may or may not have the result one would prefer: 'If we fail to speak with a man who can be spoken with, we lose a man; if we do speak with a man who cannot be spoken with, our words go for naught (子曰：可與言，而不與之言，失人；不可與言，而與不言， 失言知者不失人，以不失言)'.

Verse 10 returns to the theme of 'fear of the Lord' (see 1.7, 29; 2.5; 4.7), identifying it as the first principle (*t*ᵉ*ḥillāh*) in a definition of Wisdom. That priority also applies to the second half of the verse that identifies 'knowledge of the holy ones' (*da'ath q*ᵉ*dōšîm*) as the major source of 'understanding' (*bînāh*). In both cases the genitive construct forms are objective genitives, i.e., a person's knowledge of the divine beings. Commentators and translations mostly render the plural noun *q*ᵉ*dōšîm* as 'the Holy One', implying Yahweh, and suggest that the plural form is a 'plural of majesty', a thoroughly modern western linguistic and cultural concept that, as far as one can ascertain, had no place in ancient Israel's thought world. (The plural form *'elōhîm*, 'gods', when used for God is a carry-over from Israel's syncretistic roots—see Josh. 24.14-16)

Wisdom's gift of 'life' (*ḥayyîm*) in v. 11 is described in terms of lengthening one's lifespan, not just improving life's intrinsic value—see also 3.16. As Confucius also said: 'A person's life span depends on his uprightness' (人之生也值). The form *yôsîpû*, 'add', is third person plural, so the sense is clearly that <u>those extra days</u> will add years to one's life—the verb is active not passive.

Verse 12 offers a two-part conditional clause that, due to its brevity, is tantalizingly difficult to interpret. A contrast between the wise person and the scoffer is obvious, but the precise meaning of the phrases *ḥākamtā lᵉkā*, 'be wise to you', and *lᵉbaddᵉkā*, 'to you alone', that distinguish the wise and the scoffer are obtuse. Verse 12a seems to be saying that if one is wise then it is a personal advantage and privilege; the 'you alone' phrase in v. 12b that describes the scoffer presumably has similar but negative consequences, namely one remains a scoffer without hope of redemption. Certainty as to meaning is not possible beyond a positive outcome for the wise and a negative outcome for the fool.

9.13-18 Ms Folly

> *Ms Folly is noisy, she is ignorant(?) and does not know anything.*
> *She sits at the entrance of her house, on a seat on the high places of the town.*
> *To call to those who pass by, who are upright in their paths.*
> *'You who are simple, come on in here!' She says to the mindless one:*
> *'Stolen water is sweet, bread eaten in secret is enjoyable.'*
> *But he does not know that the dead are there, that her guests are in the depths of Sheol.*

Just as the focus of vv. 1-6 was on Lady Wisdom, these verses focus on Ms Folly. There is a deliberate pattern in the presentation of each and some repetition, as v. 14b repeats v. 3b, and v. 16 repeats v. 4.

The initial verse 13 contains two terms that are unique—*kᵉsîlût* and *pᵉtayyût* occur nowhere else in the Hebrew Bible—and the precise meaning of the latter is contested; it may derive from the root *pth* and mean 'simple', but others suggest 'seductive'. Whatever is the correct rendering, it is certainly a negative quality. Ms Folly knows nothing! She is, however, 'noisy' (*hōmiyyāh*); she makes her presence known, 'calling out' (*qr'*) invitations to naïve young men.

The imaginative poem places her at the doorway of her house (v. 14a), but then inserts the phrase that is a variant of v. 3b, a phrase that places her now on a seat (*kissē'*) on the 'heights of the town'. Does it intend to show her active all around the town? Perhaps this close repetition is an editorial link back to the initial Lady Wisdom poem rather than some additional fact about Ms Folly.

Verse 15 sets out her objective in sitting in such public spaces; it was to 'call' to any who were passing by. The participle *m^eyašš^erîm* describes morally upright individuals—*yāšār* refers to that which is straight or upright, even smooth—and their 'paths' (*'ōrḥôthām*) or manner of life in contrast to that of Ms Folly. Some read this terse phrase as descriptive of citizens going about their ordinary daily affairs rather than of their ethical living. Whatever the precise meaning, the general sense is obvious—Folly is seeking to ensnare the unwary or unsuspecting.

Verse 17 reads like a general saying with a culture-specific meaning. Folly plans to invite the naïve to enjoy 'water' and 'bread/food'. See also v. 5 and Wisdom's invitation to her feast. Both 'bread' and 'water' (rather than wine) in v. 17 have figurative meanings, namely sexual relations (5.15). The adjective 'stolen' (*g^enûbîm*) and the adverb 'secretly' (*ś^etārîm*) refer to the illicit context of the 'meal', a situation that suggests that such activity is specially pleasurable—'sweet' and 'pleasant'—as an inducement to join in.

The closing verse 18 returns to the theme of folly leading to 'death'—see 2.18 and 7.27. The concept of the 'shades' (*r^epa'îm*), Israel's ancient notion of the departed spirit, is repeated from 2.18. By locating both ends 'there', the saying links the promised 'pleasures' of Folly's house with 'death', as does the 'depths of Sheol' concept. What Folly offers is, from the Wisdom perspective, a living death, a reality unknown to, or ignored by, the one who accepts her invitation. The negated verb *yāda'* in vv. 13, 18 serves as a bracketing device for this final section.

Postscript

The Ecumenicity of Wisdom: The Book of Proverbs and Confucian Wisdom

The *Analects of Confucius* contains a treasure trove of 450 sayings attributed to this great Sage who lived for some 70 years in the region of China now known as Shandong (山東) during the mid to late 6th century BCE. His teachings, which emphasized personal morality, social relationships, and virtuous leadership, have profoundly influenced Chinese civilization and that of other East Asian cultures over the millennia.

The *Analects* speak of and advocate an ideal or culturally appropriate mode of living built around social interaction that benefits both the individual and the community, a way of living that enhances interactions across society. It has both form and substance with the Dao as the 'way' that balances both. 'If substance exceeds refinement, crudeness is the result; if refinement exceeds substance, there is superficiality; if refinement and substance are in balance, one has achieved the ideal human' (子曰：質勝文則野，文勝質則史；文質彬彬，然後君子). One who observes the Sage's advice and lives such a commendable and upright life was called 君子(*junzi*), rendered in various ways in English, but essentially one who epitomized the very best of humanity. The antithesis was called the 小人, literally the 'small person'.

The *Analects* address basic virtues such as a child's duty towards its parents (cf., Exod. 20.12), love between family members, reliability in friendships, loyalty to superiors and justice to all.: 'Great Man is conscious only of justice; Petty Man, only of self-interest.' (君子喻於義，小人喻於利). The dichotomy between the two is parallel to the biblical distinction between the wise and the fool. The use of such contrast in both traditions is a rhetorical device that is a most effective instruction format, despite appearing to be overly generalized and simplistic. Wisdom is nowhere able to demand or to call individuals to account; it can only, by example and teaching, seek to convince the community as to the merits of its practical advice.

Wisdom's instruction is always cast within a particular historical and cultural context, a context that presumably, like that of ancient Israel, has a long pre-history in which certain values had come to be recognized as important, even crucial, to its overall social order. That advice advocated a manner of living in community, as defined by its social leaders, or in this case, by Confucius and his followers. To that extent Confucian advice is similar to the contextual advice offered by Israel's ancient Sages who, along with its priests and prophets (Jer. 18.18), were one of three parties with influence in Israelite society of the time. The role of the Sage as model or teacher is vital to both traditions: 'When you see a person of the highest calibre, think of how you can emulate him. When you see someone who is not of such a calibre, examine yourself to see whether you have similar faults (見賢思齊焉；見不賢而内自省也). See Prov. 2.1-15; 4.10-15 as examples.

While it is a common Western tendency to downplay Confucian thought as 'philosophy' and elevate biblical Wisdom as 'theology', in fact both derive from exactly the same source, namely human observation, reflection on what is observed/experienced, to determine what insights might be gained thereby. Attributing the insights to divine revelation is a claim based on one's religious worldview and its preconceptions, when in fact they are a product of careful thought and reflection, true *philosophia.* The Wisdom thought-process is described perfectly in Prov. 24.30-34 and throughout Ecclesiastes (Qoheleth); it is based on human experience, both individual and communal. The resulting advice becomes integrated into each established tradition, then to be passed on to successive generations. Norms or standards for that culture are established that give it its specific identity.

Both Wisdom traditions—Confucius and ancient Israel—recognize an external 'something' that impacts on an individual's fate (命) and stamps it with authority—for Confucian thought it is 天 (Heaven), and for Israel it was a more personalized *Elohim* (God). 'Life and death are determined by fate, Riches and Honour are fixed by Heaven' (死生有命，富貴在天) relates closely to the thought in Prov. 16.9: 'The human mind plans the way, but the Lord directs the steps' (NRSV). The historical, religious and cultural contexts which shaped Wisdom's expression within each community were different, yet there remains an ecumenism in Wisdom itself by virtue of a shared humanity, resulting in parallel conclusions reached as to how to best deal with those issues that daily life presents. Confucian thought and Israelite Yahwism arose from within very different cultural settings, yet common humanity binds them together—both are concerned about 'life' (命) and how it should be lived, for Wisdom is ultimately the practical test of a tradition's worth. Biblical Wisdom was as valid for its setting as Confucius was/is for his; neither expression is exclusive, nor is one more valid or more significant than the other. To downplay the value of one tradition over that from a different culture because of one's preconceptions or vested interests is rooted in ignorance, not in Wisdom.

Reading Hebrew Wisdom materials through the prism of later Christianity's obsession with Sin, a thesis dominating the Pauline correspondence (see, e.g., Rom. 5) and associated particularly with the eleventh-century Anslem, so distorts one's reading of both biblical Wisdom and Confucius. 'Original sin' was not an ancient Israelite notion—see the testimony about Job (Job 1.1). The Hebrew concept was that despite the very real possibility of evil, humans were 'good' as created (Gen. 1.26-31). For Confucius, humans are essentially good—人本性為善. This outlook is foundational to ecumenical Wisdom.

The 'Golden Rule' is an example of advice that is common to so many human communities; it demonstrates the principle of Reciprocity. It is a principle that can keep one on the right path to the end of one's days (有一言而可以終身行之者乎). The Chinese saying, 'What you do not wish for yourself, do not unto others' (己所不慾勿施於人) equates to Prov. 24.29 that expresses the notion in a positive format, predating by centuries Jesus the Sage's reported saying, 'Do unto others as you would have others do unto you' (Mt. 7.12). Discussion as to the merits and implications of the positive version over the negative version inevitably follow, but such talk is a 'red herring'.

'Great man's attitude towards the world is such that he shows no preferences; but he is prejudiced in favour of justice' (君子之於天下也，無適 也，無莫也，義之與比). See Mic. 6.8.

'Great Man cherishes excellence; Petty Man, his own comfort. Great Man cherishes the rules and regulations; Petty Man, special favours.' (君子懷德，小人懷土； 君子懷刑，小人懷惠).

'The gentleman who prefers his own ease is no gentleman' (士而懷居，不足以為士矣).

'If the official is himself upright, the people will act accordingly without compulsion. If he is not upright, even under orders the people will not follow' (子曰：其身正，不令而行，其身不正，雖領不從).

'If an urn lacks the characteristics of an urn, how can we call it an urn' (觚不觚，觚哉觚哉！)

So many examples of the Confucian advice offered can be readily observed as similar to that found in the biblical material in terms of both its intent—social harmony and personal satisfaction—and content. Justice, compassion, considerateness, personal reputation, leadership are just some of the concerns expressed in Confucius' advice, as they are in the biblical world.

More intriguing, however, is the formal similarity of the 'numerical proverbs' in which a theme is identified, then examples listed. Proverbs 30 is one well-known biblical collection of 'numerical proverbs', including both simple and sequential (x, x+1) forms. The basic pattern followed in both traditions consists of three parts: a numeral; a title line expressing the organizing principle; the list of items that demonstrates the principle. The use of numerical forms aids memorization in a non-literate world and is a perfect teaching and learning tool. No doubt it was for that reason that in the biblical material the form was applied to other than Wisdom instruction—for example, the threats against nations in Amos 1–2.

Confucius said:

> 'The ideal human (君子) follows a three-lane path (dao 道): benevolence without concerns; wisdom that has no doubts; courage that is fearless' (君子道者三: 仁者不憂, 知(智)者不惑, 勇者不懼).
>
> 'The Master taught four things: literature, a way of life, loyalty, and faithfulness' (子以四教：文，行，忠，信)
>
> 'He who in this world practices five things may be considered benevolent (仁): humility, magnanimity, sincerity, diligence and graciousness…' (孔子曰：能行五者於天下，為仁矣… 恭，寬，信，敏，惠)
>
> 'There are nine things to which a 君子must give attention: to see when he looks; to hear when he listens; to wear a gentle expression; to have a humble attitude; to be loyal in speech; to be respectful in service; to enquire when in doubt; to think of the difficulties when angered; to think of justice when seeing advantage' (孔子曰: 君子有九思—視思明，聽思聰，色思溫，貌思恭，言思忠，事思敬，疑思問，忿思難，見得思義).

Both Wisdom collections advocate pursuit of those personal qualities that make for a refined character and enhanced inter-personal relations—the pursuit of love, wisdom, courage, humility, faithfulness, graciousness, loyalty, truthfulness, kindness, along with warnings as to the dangers of failing to live by those qualities that put at risk community harmony arising from foolish/wicked behaviour. They oppose laziness, partiality in dealings, sexual misconduct, boasting, injustice, greed and self-serving.

Furthermore, the goals advocated by Wisdom are attainable by any who are so minded; good instruction and a student's devoted attention can and should result in one attaining the ideal as intended in each culture. Confucius believed that to attain the realm of 君子 was possible: 'Benevolence is no remote ideal! We have only to desire it and we can achieve it' (子曰：仁乎遠哉？我欲仁，斯仁至矣). Each Wisdom 'school' is confident of success if its advocated values are adopted and followed as a 'path'—'path' and 'way' (dao 道) being figures that both traditions use to speak of 'life/manner of living'. Folly or being a 小人is not inherent, as one can learn Wisdom and grow to full personhood (君子) by walking that path. In fact, for Confucius, once having 'understood' (聞) the Dao, one can happily die! (子曰：朝聞道，夕死可矣). Or as Prov. 8.35 states: 'Whoever finds me, finds life'.

In seeking a theology that is comprehensive and meaningful for the Chinese churches wherever located, the work of Confucius and others in his tradition provide one key to finding an indigenous voice. The same principle applies in the West where a dominant Christian so-called 'biblical theology', dependent on the notion of God working out his salvific purposes from Adam's 'fall' to Jesus' rescue, has imposed a teleological narrative of divine rescue upon the Hebrew Bible, bypassing the ahistorical Wisdom material. That Christian reading is so alien to ancient Israel's understanding of its Scriptures. Not only is it an imported and skewed reading, it neglects and down-plays Wisdom's ecumenical advice as found in the life of Jesus the Sage, stripping him of his essential humanity in favour of a subsequent Greco-Roman Christology. Wisdom in the Hebrew Bible has to be read from the perspective of those to whom it belongs, not from an imported, and essentially Pauline, late 1st century CE, reading. Failing to honour Wisdom's contribution to a more comprehensive theology demeans both Wisdom and Theology.

Select Bibliography

Anderson, B.W., *Contours of Old Testament Theology* (Minneapolis: Fortress Press, 1999).

McKane, W., *Prophets and Wise Men* (SBT, 44: London, 1965).

Ogden, G.S., 'Numerical Sayings in Israelite Wisdom and in Confucius', *TJT* 3 (1981), pp. 145-76.

Ogden, G.S., 'Biblical and Confucian Thought: A Consideration of Some Common Teachings', *TJT* 4 (1982), pp. 215-27.

Reyburn, W.D., and E. McG. Fry, *A Handbook on Proverbs* (UBS Handbook Series; New York: United Bible Societies, 2000).

Trible, P., 'Wisdom Builds a Poem: The Architecture of Proverbs 1:20-33', *JBL* 94 (1975), pp. 509-18.

Waltke. B.K., and M. O'Connor, *An Introduction to Biblical Hebrew Syntax* (Winona Lake, IN: Eisenbrauns, 1990).

Ware, J. R., *The Sayings of Confucius* (Taipei, Confucius Publishing Co., 1977).

Whybray, R.N., *Proverbs* (NCBC; London: Marshall Pickering, 1994).

www.ingramcontent.com/pod-product-compliance
Lightning Source LLC
Chambersburg PA
CBHW061420300426
44114CB00015B/2003
9781914490712